# Dressing & Cooking
# WILD GAME

CREATIVE
PUBLISHING
international

MINNETONKA, MINNESOTA

CREATIVE PUBLISHING international

*President/CEO:* David D. Murphy

## DRESSING & COOKING WILD GAME

*Text Author and Recipe Editor:* Teresa Marrone
*Recipes and Consultation on Text:* Annette and Louis Bignami, Joan Cone, Billy Joe Cross, William Gregoire, George and Kathryn Halazon, Jim Schneider, Bill Stevens, Teresa Marrone
*Executive Editor, Outdoor Products Group:* Don Oster
*Copy Editor:* Janice Cauley
*Art Director:* Joe Fahey
*Managing Editor:* Jill Anderson
*Photographers:* Tony Kubat, John Lauenstein, Mark Macemon, Mette Nielsen, Rex Irmen, William Lindner
*Contributing Photographers:* Erwin Bauer, Albert W. Damon III, Daniel Halsey, Jerry Robb, Norm and Sil Strung
*Food Stylists:* Bobbette Destiche, Teresa Ernst, Suzanne Finley, Melinda Hutchison, Robin Krause, Lynn Lohmann, Sue Sinon, Susan Zechmann, Lynn Bachman, Carol Grones
*Deer Illustration:* Mary Albury-Noyes
*Nutritional Analysis:* Hill Nutrition
*Manager, Production Services:* Kim Gerber
*Production Manager:* Helga Thielen
*Cooperating Agencies and Individuals:* Catherine E. Adams, United States Dept. of Agriculture; Mike Barron; Browning; Coleman Co., Inc./Western Cutlery; Mary Ebnet, Wild Acres Game Farm; Federal Cartridge Corporation; Dick Grzywinski; Alan and Debbie Hart; Minnesota Department of Natural Resources – Mike Hammer, Jim Konrad, Paul Rice; Pete Nelson, Lindstrom Community Market; Larry Nelson; Remington Arms Company, Inc.; John Schneider;

Simmons Outdoor Corporation; Bob and Karen Swanson; Marsh Lake Hunting Preserve

*Printed on American paper by:* R. R. Donnelley & Sons Co.
10 9 8 7 6 5 4 3 2 1

Copyright © 2000, 1987 by Creative Publishing international, Inc.
5900 Green Oak Drive
Minnetonka, MN 55343
1-800-328-3895
All rights reserved
Printed in U.S.A.

ISBN 0-86573-108-x

**Books available from the publisher:** *The Art of Freshwater Fishing, The New Cleaning & Cooking Fish, Fishing With Live Bait, Largemouth Bass, Panfish, The Complete Guide to Hunting, Fishing With Artificial Lures, Successful Walleye Fishing, Smallmouth Bass, Freshwater Gamefish of North America, Trout, Fishing Rivers & Streams, Fishing Tips & Tricks, White-tailed Deer, Northern Pike & Muskie, All-Time Favorite Fish Recipes, The Art of Fly Tying, America's Favorite Wild Game Recipes, Advanced Bass Fishing, Upland Game Birds, North American Game Animals, North American Game Birds, Advanced Whitetail Hunting, Understanding Whitetails, Fly-Fishing Equipment & Skills, Fishing Nymphs, Wet Flies & Streamers, Fly-Tying Techniques & Patterns, Fishing Dry Flies, Bowhunting Equipment & Skills, Wild Turkey, Muzzleloading, Duck Hunting, Venison Cookery, Game Bird Cookery, Fly Fishing for Trout in Streams, Fishing for Catfish, Modern Methods of Ice Fishing*

2

# Contents

# Introduction

With increasing availability of farm-raised birds and venison in supermarkets and specialty shops, game is on the menu more than ever. Elegant game dinners command high prices at trendy restaurants. And as the popularity of farm-raised game increases, hunters find that the truly wild game they take in the field is appreciated by more people. Unlike domestic animals, wild game has never been fed with chemicals, nor is it exposed to dangerous bacteria like so much commercial poultry and livestock. Wild game truly is a priceless treat.

But game dinners often fall short of their potential. Fearing a "wild" taste, many cooks soak the meat in saltwater and prepare it with strong seasonings that disguise the natural flavor. Or, they prepare it like domestic meat and are disappointed when it comes out tough and dry. And if the game has been handled improperly in the field, it may have an off-taste regardless of how well it is prepared.

This book will help you avoid these pitfalls. The first chapter shows you how to care for every kind of game after it's down. You'll learn how to field-dress and transport big game, and how to hang, age and skin it. The section on butchering and boning big game features complete yet concise step-by-step photos that teach you to process your own game, assuring that you get exactly what you want from your big-game harvest.

You'll also find step-by-step directions for dressing and portioning small game, upland game birds, and waterfowl. Everything is covered, from wet- and dry-plucking birds to skinning squirrels. The chapter concludes with a comprehensive guide to freezing wild game that shows proven ways of packaging to prevent freezer burn, including techniques for water-packing game and wrapping odd-shaped cuts like ribs.

The chapter on cooking big game features more than 50 tempting recipes, including time-tested favorites like chicken-fried venison steak and big-game pot roast, as well as heritage recipes for corned big game, big-game mincemeat, and big-game sausage. Helpful photo sequences make it easy to butterfly steaks, prepare a rolled, stuffed venison roast, or bake a tasty big-game pie.

The next three chapters cover mouth-watering recipes for small game, upland birds, and waterfowl. You'll learn how to pressure-cook rabbits and squirrels so the meat is tender and delicious, as well as how to roast a goose with baked apples and even how to barbecue partridge on a rotisserie.

There are also recipes for sauces, stuffings, and marinades to complement game dishes. An instructive section shows you how to get the most from your game by making stock from the bones. The final chapter covers hot- and cold-smoking techniques, including a method for making traditional venison jerky.

Every recipe in this book has been thoroughly tested by professional home economists. The recipe styles range from traditional to contemporary, but all have one thing in common: they highlight the natural, distinctive flavor of the game. Throughout the book, you'll notice icons that let you find at a glance recipes that are low-fat, or are particularly quick and easy to prepare.

FAST (30 to 45 minutes for preparation and cooking)

VERY FAST (30 minutes or less for preparation and cooking)

LOW-FAT (10 or fewer grams of fat per serving)

Because wild game is harder to come by than domestic meat (and purchased farm-raised game is expensive), it pays to prepare it with the finest ingredients available. If fresh herbs are available, substitute them for the dried herbs listed, simply doubling the amount. And when a recipe calls for wine, use a good table wine. If you prefer to make the recipes non-alcoholic, use broth or water instead.

Reading through this book before your next hunt and referring to it in seasons to come is sure to help you make the most of your wild harvest. The savory game dishes you prepare will be as memorable as the hunts that made them possible.

# Field Dressing Wild Game

HUNTING KNIVES include general-purpose types, such as (1) folding drop-point and (2) folding clip-point. The tip of a clip-point is more acute and curves up higher than that of a drop-point; see inset photo, opposite page.

Special-purpose types include (3) folding bird knife, with a hook for field-dressing birds, as shown on page 38; (4) folding combination knife, with a blunt-tip blade for slitting abdomens without puncturing intestines, a clip-point

# Selecting & Sharpening Hunting Knives

A good hunting knife is one of the best investments a hunter can make. Properly selected, used, and cared for, it may well outlive him. A cheap knife, on the other hand, may not last a single hunting season.

When selecting a hunting knife, look closely at the materials, blade length and shape, and workmanship.

The blade steel should be stainless, hard but not brittle. A blade with a *Rockwell hardness rating* of 57 to 60 is hard enough to hold an edge, but soft enough for easy resharpening at home when it does become dull.

The handle should be made of hardwood, plastic-impregnated wood, or a tough synthetic. These materials last longer than brittle plastic, or than wood you can easily dent with your fingernail.

Select a knife that feels comfortable in your hand. Remember that your hands may be wet when you're using it, and look for a handle shape that's easy to hold firmly. A blade between 3½ and 4½ inches long is adequate for either big or small game.

*How to Sharpen a Knife*

SELECT a medium whetstone at least as long as the blade. (If the blade is extremely dull, use a coarse stone first, then the medium stone.) Place the stone on a folded towel for stability, and apply a little honing oil.

HOLD the base of the blade against the whetstone at the angle at which the blade was originally sharpened (usually between 12 and 17 degrees). Using moderate pressure, push the knife away from you in a smooth arc from base to tip, as if shaving thin pieces off the face of the stone. Keep the edge of the blade at the same angle, in constant contact with the whetstone. Repeat this pushing motion two more times.

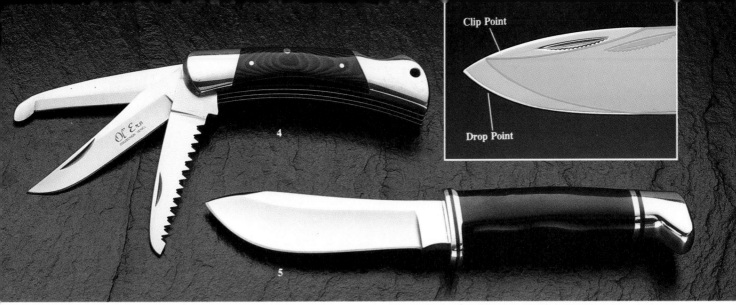

Clip Point

Drop Point

blade, and a saw for cutting through the breastbones and pelvic bones of big game; and (5) big-game skinner, whose blade has a blunt tip to avoid punching holes in the hide. The sides of the skinner blade are *concave,* curving

*Clip-point* and *drop-point* knives (see inset photo above) are good all-purpose types. The acutely pointed tip of a clip-point is good for delicate cutting, and penetrates the abdominal skin easily in field dressing. The tip of a drop-point is less apt to puncture the intestines when slitting the abdominal skin, or to punch a hole in the hide should you use it for skinning.

For convenience and safety in the field, many hunters prefer folding knives. They are shorter and easier to carry than a straight knife, and the folded blade is safely out of the way in the event of a fall. Choose folding knives carefully, checking for quality construction. When fully opened, the blade should lock in position with no trace of wiggle or

down to a thin edge that's ideal for skinning but prone to chipping when used to cut against wood or bone. The other blades shown have sides that slant down straight, with thicker, sturdier edges.

sloppiness, and the back of the blade should line up exactly with the back edge of the handle.

Use your knife only for its intended purpose. If you use it to hack wood or pry the lid off a jar, you could destroy the edge. Be sure your knife is clean and dry before you store it at the end of the season. Over time, even modern stainless steel can be corroded by salts or acids.

A sharp blade is safer than a dull one. It gives you more control, and you need less pressure to get the job done. Dress the edge often with a sharpening steel (page 21). A steel does not remove metal from the blade, but simply realigns the edge. When the blade becomes so dull that the steel won't dress it, sharpen it with a whetstone.

DRAW the knife toward you in an arc three times, maintaining the same angle. Continue sharpening alternate sides, adding oil if necessary, until the blade hangs up when drawn very gently over a fingernail.

REPEAT the previous steps on a fine whetstone. If the stone clogs, wipe and re-oil it. The knife is sharp when it slices effortlessly through a piece of paper. Clean the whetstone with soapy water for storage.

HANDY sharpening devices include (1) pre-angled sharpening kits; (2) ceramic sticks, which have a light sharpening action; and (3) diamond-impregnated sticks, which remove as much metal as a medium stone.

# Big Game:
# Field Dressing
# & Transport

A little homework before a big-game hunt can save a lot of time and effort once you've bagged your animal. And it will insure that the meat you bring home will be in prime condition for the table.

Familiarize yourself with state and local regulations. Some states prohibit quartering and skinning in the field; others require that you turn in certain parts for biological study. Be sure to check the regulations booklet available with your license. For more information, contact state or federal wildlife-management agencies.

If you are hunting for a trophy, consult in advance with a reliable taxidermist. He can give you advice on the best ways to handle the head and antlers in the field. There are also several good do-it-yourself kits for antler mounting and hide tanning.

The hides of deer, moose, and elk make excellent leather. Many tanneries will buy raw hides directly from hunters. If you plan on selling the hide, find out how the buyer wants it prepared. Some tanneries will exchange a raw hide for a pair of finished leather gloves. Or, you may want to have the hide tanned and returned to you.

Unless you have a reliable cold-storage area for holding your animal prior to butchering, make arrangements with a locker plant before you hunt. Ask about the locker's business hours; you don't want to return from hunting on a warm Saturday only to discover the plant is closed for the weekend.

HANG field-dressed big game in a tree to speed its cooling. Hanging also helps protect it from scavenging animals if you must leave to get help carrying it out. Use a block and tackle (inset) for easier lifting.

10

EQUIPMENT for field dressing includes: (1) folding lock-back knife and a spare, (2) small whetstone or sharpening stick, (3) several foot-long pieces of kitchen string, (4) two clean sponges, (5) zip-lock plastic bags, (6) rubber gloves, (7) block and tackle, and (8) 20 feet of ¼-inch nylon rope. If hunting moose or elk, also bring (9) cloth bags for carrying out the quarters if skinned, and (10) a belt axe or folding game saw for quartering. Hooks (11) can be slipped over the edges of the split ribcage, then tied to trees to hold the body open while gutting. Stow everything but the belt axe in your pack, along with a first-aid kit and other hunting gear.

## In the Field

Before you shoot, consider the location and body position of the animal. Remember that you'll have to get it out of the area after it's down. If you spot an animal across a canyon, consider possible drag routes before shooting. A moose standing in a bog may be a tempting target, but you would probably need several people to move it to dry land for field dressing and quartering.

Shot placement affects both the quality and quantity of the meat you bring home. A study at Texas A&M University showed that game killed instantly with a clean shot produces meat more tender and flavorful than game only wounded with the first shot. Game animals, like humans, produce adrenalin and other chemicals when frightened or stressed. These chemicals make the meat tough and gamey. A poorly placed shot may also damage choice cuts, or rupture the stomach or intestines, tainting the meat.

If possible, shoot an animal that's standing still rather than running. A shot in the heart or neck will drop it instantly, and you'll lose little meat.

Approach a downed animal with caution, keeping your gun loaded and staying away from the hooves and antlers. Nudge the animal with your foot, or gently touch your gun barrel to its eye. If there's any reaction, shoot it in the head or heart. When certain the animal is dead, unload your gun and place it safely out of the way.

Field-dress the animal immediately to drain off the blood and dissipate the body heat. Wear rubber gloves to protect you from any parasites or blood-borne diseases the animal may be carrying, and to make cleanup easier.

The step-by-step instructions on the following pages will guide you through a field-dressing procedure that produces a clean carcass. Splitting the pelvis is optional with this method. In warm weather, you may wish to split the pelvis, because the hams cool faster when separated. However, an animal with a split pelvis is more difficult to drag. The separated hind legs flop around, and the cavity may get dirty.

If you elect to split the pelvis, cut between the hams as described. Then, locate the natural seam between the two halves of the pelvic bone, and cut through it with your knife. On a large or old animal, you may need to use a game saw or hatchet. Some hunters stand their knife upright with its tip on the seam, then strike the knife with their palm to split the pelvis. Do not attempt this unless you have a sturdy knife; you could damage the blade.

Be sure to follow state regulations requiring evidence of the sex left on the carcass. Antlers are usually adequate to identify a buck; in some states, antlers must be a certain length for the animal to be legal.

Where the law allows, attach the registration tag after field dressing, rather than before. The tag may get ripped off during the dressing procedure.

11

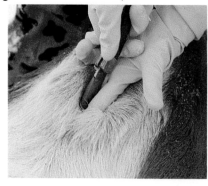

1. LOCATE the base of the breastbone by pressing on the center of the ribcage until you feel its end. Make a shallow cut that is long enough to insert the first two fingers of your left hand. Be careful not to puncture the intestines when cutting.

2. FORM a V with the first two fingers of your left hand. Hold the knife between your fingers with the cutting edge up, as shown. Cut through the abdominal wall to the pelvic area. Your fingers prevent you from puncturing the intestines.

3. SEPARATE the external reproductive organs of a buck from the abdominal wall, but do not cut them off completely. Remove the udder of a doe if it was still nursing. The milk sours rapidly, and could give the meat an unpleasant flavor.

14. SPONGE cavity clean, and prop open with a stick. If the urinary tract or intestines have been severed, wash meat with snow or clean water. If you must leave the animal, drape it over brush or logs with the cavity down, or hang it from a tree to speed cooling.

Anatomy of a Male Whitetail Deer

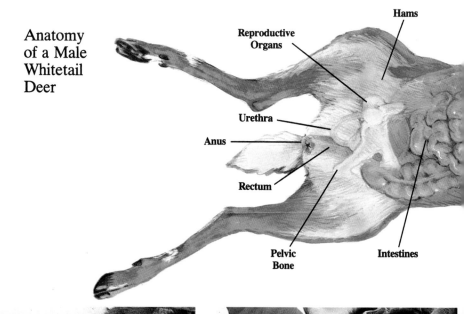

Reproductive Organs

Hams

Urethra

Anus

Rectum

Pelvic Bone

Intestines

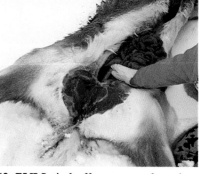

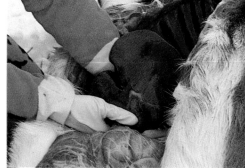

13. GRASP the windpipe and esophagus firmly. Pull down and away from the animal's body. If the organs do not pull away freely, the diaphragm may still be partially attached. Scoop from both ends toward the middle to finish rolling out the entrails.

12. PULL tied-off rectum and urethra underneath the pelvic bone and into the body cavity, unless you have split the pelvic bone. (If you have, this is unnecessary.) Roll the animal on its side so the entrails begin to spill out the side of the body cavity.

11. CUT the tubes that attach the liver and remove it. Check liver for spots, cysts, or scarring, which could indicate parasites or disease. If you see any, discard the liver. If liver is clean, place into plastic bag with heart. Place on ice as soon as possible.

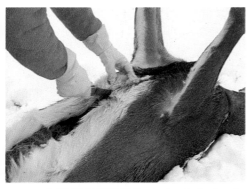

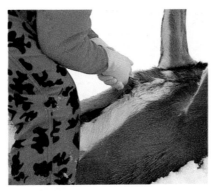

4. STRADDLE the animal, facing its head. Unless you plan to mount the head, cut the skin from the base of the breastbone to the jaw, with the cutting edge of the knife up. If you plan to mount the head, follow your taxidermist's instructions.

5. BRACE your elbows against your legs, with your left hand supporting your right. Cut through the center of the breastbone, using your knees to provide leverage. If the animal is old or very large, you may need to use a game saw or small axe.

6. SLICE between the hams to free a buck's urethra, or if you elect to split the pelvic bone on either a buck or doe. Make careful cuts around the urethra until it is freed to a point just above the anus. Be careful not to sever the urethra.

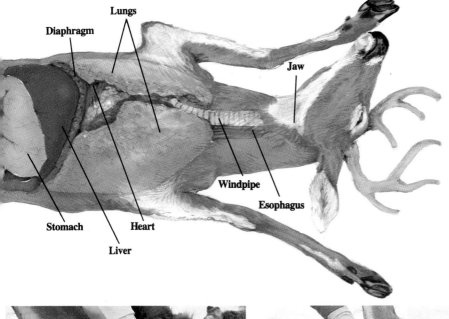

Lungs

Diaphragm

Jaw

Windpipe

Esophagus

Stomach          Heart

Liver

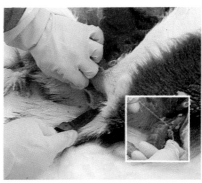

7. CUT around the anus; on a doe, the cut should also include the reproductive opening (above the anus). Free the rectum and urethra by loosening the connective tissue with your knife. Tie off the rectum and urethra with kitchen string (inset).

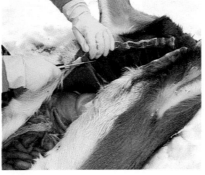

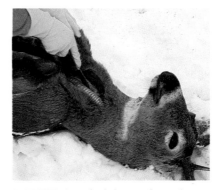

10. REMOVE the heart by severing the connecting blood vessels. Hold the heart upside down for a few moments to drain excess blood. Place heart in a plastic bag. Some hunters find it easier to remove the entrails first, then take the heart and liver from the gutpile.

9. HOLD ribcage open on one side with left hand. Cut the diaphragm, from the rib opening down to the backbone. Stay as close to the ribcage as possible; do not puncture the stomach. Repeat on other side so the cuts meet over the backbone.

8. FREE the windpipe and esophagus by cutting the connective tissue. Sever windpipe and esophagus at the jaw. Grasp them firmly and pull down, continuing to cut where necessary, until freed to the point where the windpipe branches out into the lungs.

## Transporting Big-Game Animals

After field dressing, move the animal to camp as soon as possible. Leave the hide on to protect the meat from dirt and flies. The hide will also prevent the surface from drying too much during aging (page 17). In hot weather, however, you may want to remove the hide in the field to help cool the carcass.

If you plan to skin the animal in the field, bring along a large cloth bag or sheet to keep the meat clean during transport. Never put the carcass or quarters in plastic bags unless the meat is thoroughly chilled. The plastic traps the body heat, and the meat may be ruined. Avoid plastic garbage bags; they may be treated with a toxic disinfectant.

You may have to quarter an elk or moose to transport it from the field (opposite page). Some hunters skin the animal before quartering, so the hide can be tanned in one piece. Others prefer to quarter the animal first. A quartered hide is still suitable for tanning; in fact, most tanneries split whole elk or moose hides in half to make them easier to handle.

Wear blaze-orange clothing and make lots of noise when you move an animal in the field. Hunters have been known to mistakenly shoot at animals being dragged or carried. For this reason, the traditional method of carrying a deer, by lashing it to a pole between two hunters, is not recommended. If you must carry an animal this way, drape it completely with blaze-orange cloth.

Once in camp, hang the animal up (pages 16-17). Hanging aids cooling and blood drainage, and the stretching helps tenderize the meat. Clean the clots and excess blood from the heart and liver, then place them in plastic bags on ice.

Ideally, the carcass should be cooled to 40°F within 24 hours. Cool it as rapidly as possible, but don't allow it to freeze. The meat loses moisture if frozen and thawed, and the carcass is difficult to skin when frozen even partially. If the days are warm and the nights cool, keep the carcass covered with a sleeping bag during the day. If the nights are warm as well, store the carcass at a locker plant.

The best way to transport the animal home is in a closed trailer or covered pickup. In cool, dry weather, you can carry an animal on top of your car, with the head forward. Do not carry an animal on the hood, because heat from the engine will spoil the meat. If your trip is long and hot, pack bags of dry ice around the carcass. Or, quarter the animal, wrap well in plastic, and pack it into coolers with ice. Be sure to check state laws regarding transport of big game.

DRAG a deer with each front leg tied to an antler to keep from snagging brush. If the deer is antlerless, tie a rope around the neck. Snow makes dragging easier. If the terrain is dusty, sew the carcass shut with a cord after punching a hole in each side of the rib cage. A bear may be dragged on a heavy tarp, to avoid damaging the fur.

PILE quarters onto a horse, all-terrain vehicle, or snowmobile. Skinned quarters should be wrapped in cloth bags. Quarters from smaller animals can be strapped to a pack frame and packed out one at a time. If the quarters have not been skinned and the terrain is smooth, they can be dragged out as shown on the opposite page.

*How to Quarter an Elk or Moose (pictured: Elk)*

BEND a leg sharply, then cut the skin around the joint to remove the lower leg. Repeat on all legs.

SAW off the head after skinning the neck area. Sawing it before skinning would force hair into the meat.

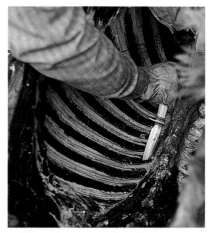

CUT between the third and fourth ribs, from the backbone to the tips of the ribs. Cut from inside the body.

SEPARATE the front half of the animal from the rear half by sawing through the backbone.

SPLIT the hide along the backbone on both halves, then peel it back several inches on each side of the cut.

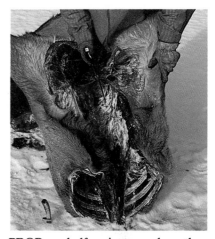

PROP one half against your legs, then begin sawing lengthwise through the backbone.

CONTINUE cutting while keeping the back off the ground. Gravity will help pull the quarters apart, making the cutting easier. Your saw will not bind, as it would if the half were lying on the ground.

QUARTERED elk looks like this. Depending on the animal's size, elk quarters weigh 60 to 125 pounds each; moose, up to 225 pounds. Where the law allows, some hunters bone the animal in the field to reduce weight.

DRAG out a hindquarter by punching a hole behind the last rib, then threading a rope through and tying as pictured. This way, you drag with the grain of the hair. To drag out a forequarter, tie a rope tightly around the neck.

# Hanging, Aging, & Skinning Big Game

How should I hang my animal — from the head or by the hind legs? And what about aging — does it improve the meat or spoil it? If I'm going to age the animal, should I leave the hide on during aging or take it off? These questions cause a great deal of debate among hunters.

If you want the head for a trophy, the first question is answered for you: the animal must be hung by the hind legs. Many hunters hang all big game this way, and the U.S. Department of Agriculture recommends this method for butchering beef. Hanging by the hind legs allows the blood to drain from the choice hindquarters. If your animal must be hung outdoors, however, it's better to hang it from the head because of the direction of hair growth. Otherwise, the upturned hair would trap rain and snow.

Many laboratory and taste tests have demonstrated that aging will definitely tenderize the meat. The special tenderness and flavor of beef prime rib result from extended aging. Wild game can benefit in the same way. It's a matter of personal taste: some prefer the aged flavor and tenderness, others don't. Aging is unnecessary if all the meat will be ground into sausage or burger.

*How to Hang an Animal by the Hind Legs (pictured: Deer)*

MAKE a *gambrel* out of a 3-foot-long 2 × 2. Cut a shallow notch all around the wood an inch from each end, and another in the middle.

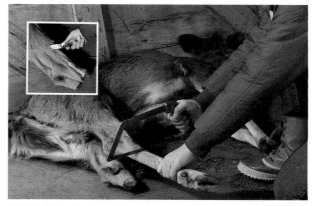

SAW off the bottom of each hind leg several inches below the knee. Cutting from inside the skin, slit the skin on each leg to a point about 4 inches above the knee (inset).

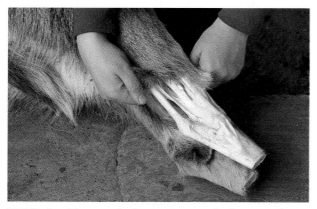

PEEL the skin over the leg to uncover the large tendon at the back of the leg. Then slit any tissue between the bone and the large tendon. The tendon is needed for hanging the animal, so be careful not to sever it.

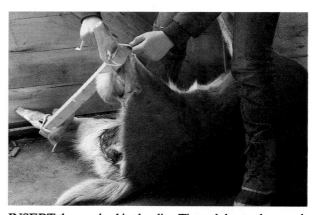

INSERT the gambrel in the slits. Tie each leg to the wood, wrapping the rope in the notch. Tie 6 feet of rope to the center notch, then loop it over a sturdy beam or through a pulley. Hoist the deer completely off the ground.

To prevent unwanted bacterial growth during the aging process, the carcass temperature must be stabilized between 35° and 40°F. If it fluctuates widely, condensation may form. Temperatures above 40° promote excess bacterial growth and cause the fat to turn rancid. If you age the animal outdoors or in a shed, be prepared to butcher it immediately or take it to a locker should the weather turn warm.

Leave the hide on during aging, if possible. It helps stabilize the temperature of the meat, and also reduces dehydration. In a study at the University of Wyoming, an elk carcass was cut in half down the backbone; one half was skinned, the other was not. After two weeks of aging, the skinned side lost over 20 percent more moisture. Animals aged without the hide will have a great deal of dried, dark meat to be trimmed, further reducing your yield.

During aging, enzyme activity breaks down the connective tissue that makes meat tough. Elk has more connective tissue than deer, antelope, or bear, and

can be aged longer. Antelope is probably the most tender of these animals; extended aging may give it a mushy texture. Many people prefer their antelope aged only about 3 days. Bear can age from 3 days to a week. Deer and cow elk reach their prime in a week to 10 days, and bull elk require up to 14 days. These times are for *ideal* conditions. Do not attempt to age an animal in warm conditions.

Some people prefer to quarter their meat, wrap the quarters in cloth, then age them in a refrigerator or old chest-style pop cooler. The effects are almost the same as hanging a whole carcass. The meat may be slightly less tender, because it doesn't get stretched as much.

If you prefer not to age the animal, delay butchering for at least 24 hours, until the carcass has cooled and the muscles have relaxed. The cuts will be ragged and unappealing if you start before cooling is complete, and the meat will be tough if butchered while the muscles are still contracted.

## Skinning Big Game

Skinning is easiest while the animal is still warm. If you age the meat, however, it's best to leave the skin on until butchering.

Most hunters skin their animals by hand. The task isn't difficult, requiring only a knife and a saw. For easiest skinning, hang the animal from a pulley. Then you can raise or lower the carcass, so the area you're working on will always be at eye level. Or, hoist the animal on a rope running through a heavy-duty screw eye fastened to a solid ceiling beam.

Try to keep hair off the meat during skinning. Keep your knife sharp, touching it up as necessary with a steel or stone. Cut through the skin from the inside out, so your knife slips between the hairs. This way, you avoid cutting hairs in half or driving them into the meat, and your knife won't dull as quickly.

If you have several animals to skin, it may be worthwhile to set up a system for skinning with mechanical power. The photo sequence at the bottom of the opposite page shows how to skin a deer with a car. You can use the same method with a winch. But don't try to skin your animal mechanically if it's shot through the spine or neck; it could break apart.

After skinning, lay the hide out on a piece of plywood, skin side up. If you take a few moments to scrape off any bits of meat or fat, you will get a better piece of leather.

Most tanneries prefer to receive a hide salted and rolled. To protect it from rain and animals during the salting process, find a sheltered spot like a shed or garage. Sprinkle the skin side liberally with salt, and rub some into the edges, cuffs, and neck area. Tilt the plywood slightly so the hide will drain.

After a day, add more salt and fold the hide in half, skin side in. Roll the folded hide into a bundle and tie it with twine. Don't put the rolled hide in plastic, except for shipping, because it may rot. Keep it cold, and get it to the tannery as soon as possible.

If you have a deer hide, save the tail. It can be used for jig and fly tying, and hide buyers may pay several dollars for it.

If you're not going to butcher the animal yourself, deliver the carcass to the butcher with the hide still on, and let him skin it.

*How to Skin an Animal Hanging by the Hind Legs (pictured: Antelope)*

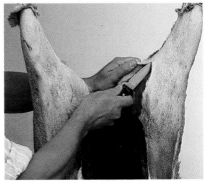

CUT the hide along the inner side of each hind leg. Note that the cut is made from the inside of the skin.

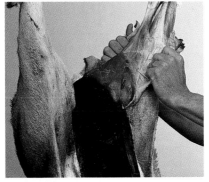

PEEL the hide away from the legs. Continue peeling until both legs are skinned and you reach the tail.

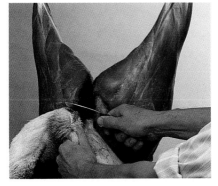

SEVER the tailbone close to the animal's rump. Leave the tailbone inside the skin.

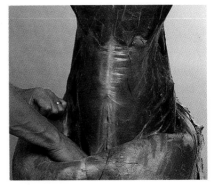

CONTINUE peeling, using your fist to free the hide along the back. Use a knife only where necessary; take care not to cut a hole in the hide.

SAW off front legs just above the joint, after cutting along the inside of each leg and peeling the hide. Keep skinning until you reach the head.

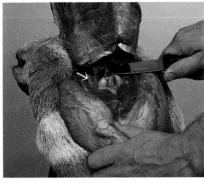

CUT off the head at the Atlas joint (arrow). First, make a deep cut around the neck at the base of the skull. Twist the head to pop the Atlas joint.

## How to Skin an Animal Hanging from the Head (pictured: Deer)

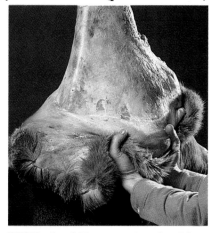

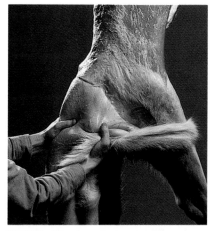

CUT the skin around the base of the head. Then peel the hide away from the neck with your fingers, using a knife only where necessary.

PEEL the hide over the shoulders. Saw off the front legs above the joint, as described on the opposite page. Pull the hide off the front legs.

KEEP skinning down to the rump. Sever the tailbone; cut off hind legs above knee. Cut hide along inside of each leg. Pull hide completely off.

## How to Skin an Animal with Mechanical Power (pictured: Deer)

HANG the animal from the head on a sturdy tree. Remove the lower portion of each leg. Cut the skin around the neck, and peel back about 6 inches. Then, cut the skin along the inside of each leg, up to the body cavity.

PLACE a golf ball or small rounded rock under the peeled neck skin. Gather the skin around it, and tie off tightly with strong cord. Fasten the cord to a secure part of a vehicle, or to a winch.

BEGIN driving slowly away from the animal. If using a winch, crank steadily. The hide will begin peeling off. If the hide seems hard to pull, you may have to start it over the shoulders by hand.

CONTINUE driving until skinning is complete. Once the hide is past the shoulders, the rest comes off easily. More fat and meat will probably remain on the hide than if you had skinned it by hand.

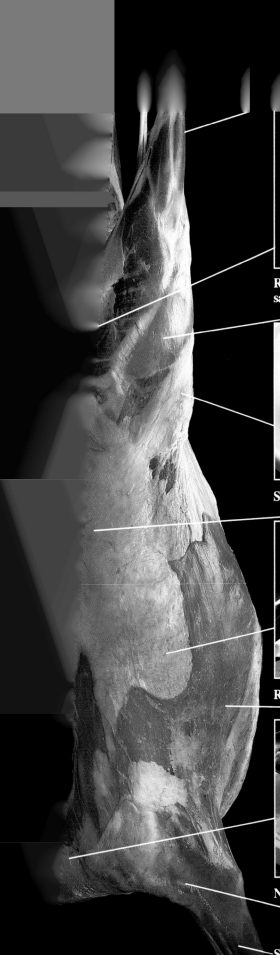

RUMP: Kabobs, steaks, roasts, sautées, grilling

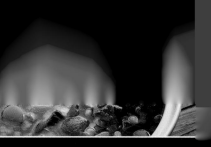

SHANK: Soups, stock, burger, sausage, jerky

BOTTOM and TOP ROUNDS: Roasts, steaks, sautées, kabobs

SIRLOIN TIP: Steaks, roasts

BACKSTRAP: Grilling, butterflied steaks, sautées

RIBS: Ribs, burger, sausage

BRISKET and TRIMMINGS: Burger, sausage, jerky, corning

SHOULDER: Jerky, pot roasts, stews, burger, sausage

NECK: Sausage, burger, pot roasts

SHANK

# Butchering Big Game

When you do your own butchering, you know that the meat has been handled with care, and you get the cuts you prefer. You will probably be willing to take more time trimming than a butcher would, so your finished cuts may have less gristle, fat, and silverskin on them.

In most cases, the animal is butchered while still hanging from the skinning process. Use caution when butchering a hanging animal. When you cut off each portion, you must "catch" it, and this can be tricky with a knife in one hand. A deer leg, for instance, may weigh 20 pounds or more, so you may need a partner to catch it. Be absolutely certain that your partner stays clear of your knife, and never allow him to cut at the same time. For safety, some hunters prefer to butcher on a large table.

The photo sequence on pages 22 and 23 shows how to cut up a deer that is hanging from the head. The procedure is somewhat different if the animal is hanging by the hind legs. You will not be able to cut off the hind legs because they are supporting the carcass. Instead, remove the front legs, backstrap, and ribs as described, then place the hindquarters on a table to finish cutting.

After cutting up the carcass, bone the meat. Boning is easier than bone-in butchering, and usually results in tastier meat. Bone marrow is fatty and can turn rancid, even in the freezer. By boning, you avoid cutting the bones, so there is no bone residue to affect the meat's flavor. In addition, boned meat takes less freezer space and is easier to wrap. There are no sharp edges to puncture the freezer wrap and expose the meat to freezer burn.

On pages 24 and 25, you'll learn an easy method for boning a big-game animal. To roughly estimate the amount of boned meat you will get, divide the field-dressed weight of your animal in half. You will get a smaller yield if the shot damaged much meat, or if you aged the animal.

Work on a large hardwood or plexiglass cutting board. To keep bacterial growth to a minimum, wash the board with a solution of 3 tablespoons of household bleach to 1 gallon of water, and wash it occasionally during the boning process. Keep two large bowls handy for the trimmings. As you bone, place large chunks to be used for stew in one bowl; small scraps for sausage or burger in the other.

How you make the final boning cuts depends on the animal's size. On a moose, for instance, the rump portion is large enough to yield several roasts. But on an antelope, the same cut is too small for a roast, and is better for steaks, kabobs, or stroganoff.

Keep the meat cool throughout the butchering and boning process. Work on the carcass in a cool shed or garage. To reduce bacterial growth, bone and freeze each portion as you remove it, or refrigerate it until you can bone it. You can butcher faster by working in pairs; while one person cuts up the carcass, the other works on boning.

Save the bones if you want to make soup or stock (pages 69 and 144). The backbone makes particularly good stock. Saw the larger bones into pieces to fit your stockpot.

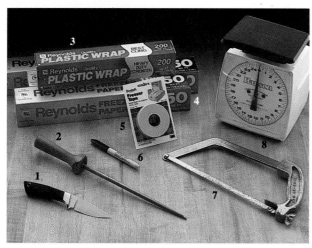

EQUIPMENT for butchering big game includes (1) hunting or boning knife, (2) sharpening steel or whetstone, (3) heavy-duty plastic wrap, (4) freezer paper, (5) freezer tape, (6) waterproof marking pen, (7) game or meat saw, (8) kitchen scale.

DRESS your knife frequently with a sharpening steel. Hold the base of the blade against the steel at the angle at which it was originally sharpened. Draw the knife toward you in an arc from base to tip. Repeat on other side. Alternate sides until the blade is sharp.

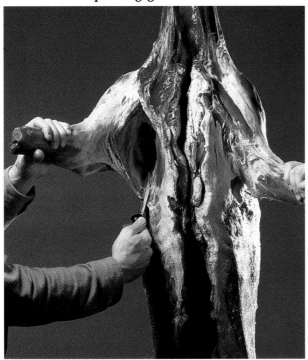

1. PUSH the front leg away from the body, then begin cutting between the leg and the ribcage. Continue until you reach the shoulder. It helps to have someone steady the carcass, but make sure he or she is safely away from your knife.

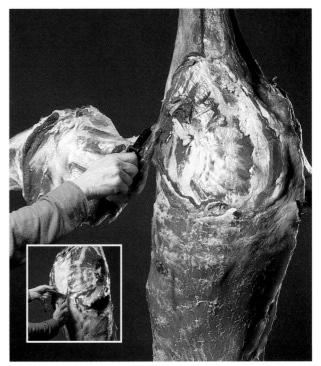

2. REMOVE the front leg by cutting between the shoulder blade and the back. Repeat with the other leg. Remove the layer of brisket meat over the ribs (inset). Moose or elk brisket is thick enough to be rolled for corning (page 85). Grind thin brisket for burger.

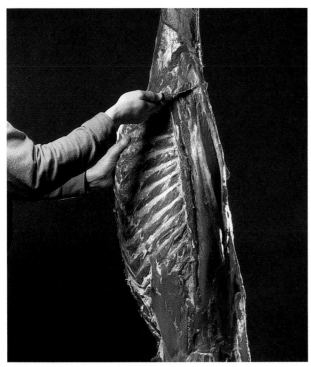

3. CUT the meat at the base of the neck to begin removing a *backstrap*. There are two backstraps, one on each side of the spine. Backstraps can be butterflied for steaks (page 53), cut into roasts, or sliced thinly for sautéeing. The lower part, or *loin*, is most tender.

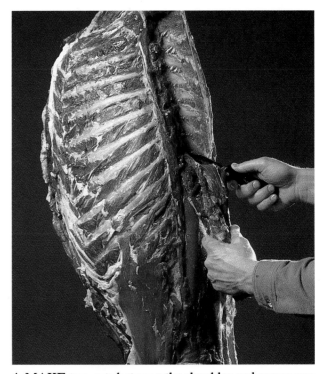

4. MAKE two cuts between the shoulder and rump: one along the spine, the other along the rib tops. Keep your knife close to the bones, removing as much meat as possible. Cut off this first backstrap at the rump, then remove the backstrap on the other side of the spine.

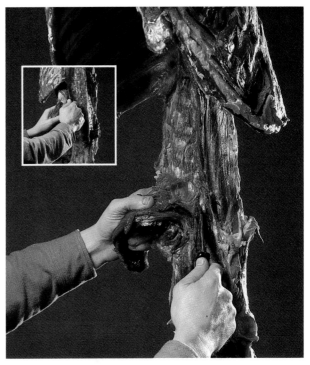

5. BEGIN cutting one hind leg away, exposing the ball-and-socket joint (arrow). Push the leg back to pop the joint apart, then cut through the joint. Work your knife around the tailbone and pelvis until the leg is removed. Repeat with the other leg.

6. CUT the *tenderloins* from inside the body cavity after trimming the flank meat below the last rib (inset). The flank meat can be ground, or cut into thin strips for jerky. Many hunters remove the tenderloins before aging the animal, to keep them from darkening and dehydrating.

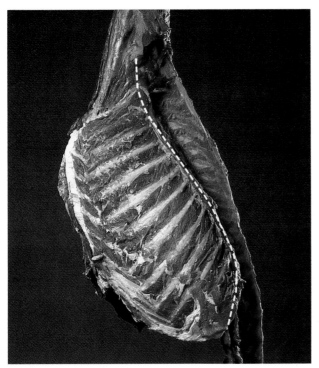

7. REMOVE the ribs if desired by sawing along the backbone (dotted lines). Cut around the base of the neck, then twist the backbone off. Separate the neck and head (page 18). Bone the neck to grind for burger, or keep it whole for pot roasting.

8. TRIM the ribs by cutting away the ridge of meat and gristle along the bottom. If the ribs are long, saw them in half. Cut ribs into racks of three or four. If you don't want to save the ribs, you can bone the meat between them and grind it for burger or sausage.

*How to Bone a Hind Leg (pictured: Antelope)*

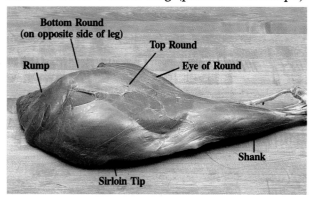

A HIND LEG consists of the sirloin tip, the top and bottom rounds, the eye of round, a portion of the rump, and the shank. The sirloin, rounds, and rump are tender cuts for roasting or grilling; the shank is tough, and best for ground meat or soups.

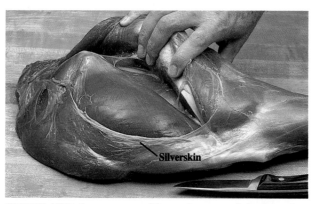

SEPARATE the *top round* from the rest of the leg after cutting through the thin layer of silverskin that covers the leg. Work your fingers into the natural seam, then begin pulling the top round away from the leg. Use your knife only where necessary to free the meat.

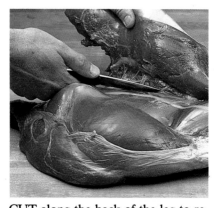

CUT along the back of the leg to remove the top round completely. The top round is excellent when butterflied, rolled and tied for roasting (see opposite page). Or, cut it into two smaller flat roasts, cube for kabobs, or slice for sautées.

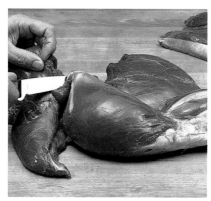

REMOVE the *rump* portion. Cut the rump off at the top of the hipbone after removing the silverskin and pulling the muscle groups apart with your fingers. A large rump is excellent for roasting; a small one can be cut for steaks, kabobs, or sautées.

CUT *bottom round* away from *sirloin tip* after turning leg over and separating these two muscle groups with your fingers. Next, carve sirloin tip away from bone. Sirloin tip makes a choice roast or steaks; bottom round is good for roasting, steaks, or kabobs.

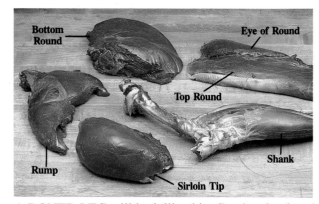

A BONED LEG will look like this. Cut the *shank* and upper leg bone apart at the knee joint if you plan on using the shank for soup. Or, cut the meat off the shank close to the bone; trim away the tendons and silverskin, and grind the meat for burger or sausage. Use the leftover bones for stock (page 144). On a larger animal, you may wish to separate the *eye of round* from the top round.

MAKE large-diameter steaks from a whole hind leg by cutting across all the muscle groups rather than boning as described above. First, remove the rump portion as described, then cut the leg into inch-thick steaks. As each steak is cut, work around the bone with a fillet knife, then slide the steak over the end of the bone. Continue steaking until you reach the shank.

## How to Bone a Front Leg (pictured: Deer)

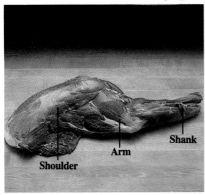

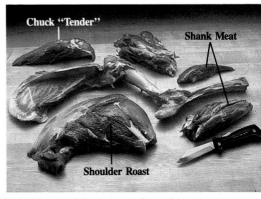

A FRONT LEG consists of the shoulder, arm, and shank. The meat from the front leg is less tender than that from the hind leg, and is used for pot roasting, stews, jerky, or grinding.

CUT along bony ridge in the middle of the shoulder blade. One side yields the small boneless chuck "tender." Bone the other side along the dotted line to make a shoulder roast.

TRIM remaining meat from bones. Use the chuck "tender" for jerky or stews. Pot roast the shoulder roast, cut into stew chunks, or use for jerky. Grind the shank meat for burger.

## How to Make a Rolled Roast (pictured: Deer Bottom Round)

BUTTERFLY meat that is thicker than one inch by cutting into two thinner pieces; leave the meat connected at one edge. Open the butterflied meat up so it lies flat. Roll the meat tightly with the grain, tucking in any irregular edges.

TIE the rolled meat about an inch from the end that is farthest from you; use a 60" length of kitchen string. Leave several inches at the short end of the string; you will need to tie the two ends of the string together after making loops around the meat.

MAKE a loop in the string, then twist the loop once to make a small "braid" (arrow). Slip the braided loop over the end of the meat closest to you, then slide the loop so it is about one inch from the string tied around the far end.

SNUG up this first loop by pulling on the long end of the string, adjusting its length so the braid lines up with the original knot. The roast will look more attractive when it is served if all the braids are lined up along the top of the roast.

CONTINUE making loops about an inch apart, snugging them up as you go. Tie on additional string if necessary. When you have made a loop about an inch from the close end (dotted line), slip the string underneath the roast so it comes out on the far side.

TIE the two ends of the string together with a double overhand knot. Trim both ends of the string close to the knot. When you are ready to carve a cooked rolled roast, simply snip the loops along the top of the roast and pull off the string.

# Dressing Small Game

Proper field care of small game ensures excellent eating. Field-dress rabbits, hares, and squirrels as soon as possible, or the delicately flavored meat may pick up an unpleasant taste. Squirrel seems particularly susceptible to off-tastes, so knowledge-able hunters take time to field-dress squirrels im-mediately after shooting. Most raccoon hunters skin and dress their raccoons at home shortly after the hunt. Raccoon meat doesn't suffer from the minor delay, and the pelt is more valuable if it hasn't been cut for field-dressing.

A great deal has been written about small game transmitting diseases to humans. Such diseases are contracted by handling entrails or uncooked meat from infected animals. Bacteria passes through cuts in a person's skin or through the mucous membranes. But infected animals are rarely encountered, because the diseases usually kill them or weaken them so much that predators can easily capture them.

To avoid any danger, never shoot an animal that moves erratically or otherwise appears sick. Wear rubber gloves when dressing or skinning any small game. Never touch your mouth or eyes, and wash your hands thoroughly when finished. Dispose of the entrails and skin in a spot where dogs and cats can't reach them and become infected. For safer disposal, some hunters carry plastic bags.

When field-dressing small game, you may encoun-ter various internal parasites. Most of these, while visually unappealing, do not harm the meat and are removed during dressing or skinning.

Raccoon populations in some areas of the country carry a roundworm that may be found in the drop-pings and on the pelt. In very rare circumstances, this parasite can be transmitted to humans. Although the possibility of contamination is slim, raccoon hunters should wear rubber gloves while dressing and skinning.

When handling rabbits, wear the gloves not only for dressing and skinning, but also during all stages of kitchen preparation. Rabbits occasionally carry *tula-remia,* a bacterial disease that can be transmitted to humans. Thorough cooking destroys the bacteria.

After dressing, small-game animals must be cooled properly. Don't put them in a hot car or carry them for hours in the pocket of your hunting coat. In-stead, leave them in a shaded spot, out of the reach of predators. Some hunters hang their field-dressed animals in a shady tree, so the carcasses can drain as well as cool. Never put an animal in a plastic bag until it's completely cooled.

In warm weather, it's best to chill the dressed ani-mals in a cooler. Reusable plastic ice packs are better than plain ice, since they won't fill the cooler with melted water. Plastic pop bottles filled with water and then frozen work well also.

Before skinning, try to determine the animal's age, because this may affect the way you cook it. The tail of a young squirrel tapers to a point, while the tail of an old one is the same width throughout. A young rabbit has soft, flexible ears and a small cleft in the upper lip; an old one has stiffer ears, often with white edges, and a deeply cleft upper lip. In all kinds of small game, the meat of old animals is darker in color. Also, the teeth darken and dull with age, and the claws become blunt.

## How to Field-dress Small Game

EQUIPMENT for field-dressing small game includes (1) hunting knife, (2) rubber gloves, (3) plastic bags, (4) paper towels, (5) cord for hanging dressed animals in a tree.

MAKE a shallow cut (dotted line) from the vent to the rib cage. Be sure not to puncture the intestines. Some hunters extend the cut through the rib cage to the neck.

PULL OUT all the entrails. Check a rabbit's liver for white spots indicating disease; if it's clean, save it in a plastic bag with the heart. Wipe cavity with paper towels.

## How to Skin a Rabbit or Hare

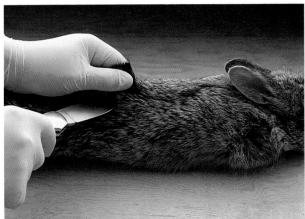

PINCH the hide up and away from the middle of the rabbit's spine. Slit the hide from the spine down the sides, being careful not to cut the meat.

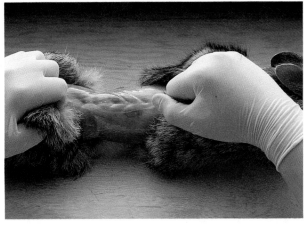

GRASP the hide with both hands and pull in opposite directions. Keep pulling until all the legs are skinned up to the feet.

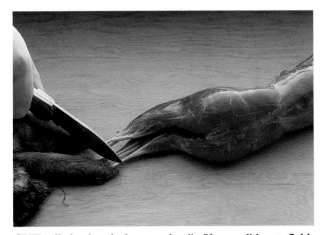

CUT off the head, feet, and tail. If you did not field-dress the rabbit before skinning, slit the underside from vent to neck, then remove all internal organs. Save liver and heart if desired.

CLEAN body cavity, removing any material left after dressing. Rinse briefly under running water and pat dry. Squirrels can also be skinned this way, but not as easily (see page 28 for an easier squirrel-skinning method).

*How to Skin a Squirrel*

CUT through the base of the tailbone, starting on the underside of the tail. Stop when the bone is severed; do not cut the skin on the top side of the tail.

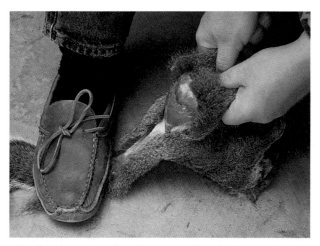

PLACE the squirrel on the ground, and set your foot on the base of the tail. Pull up on the rear legs, peeling the skin all the way to the front legs.

PEEL the "britches" off the rear legs to the ankle joints. Keep your foot firmly on the base of the tail until all skinning is complete.

REMOVE the squirrel's back feet by cutting through the ankle joints with a knife or game shears. If using a knife, cut away from yourself as pictured.

PULL each front leg out of the skin, as far as the wrist joint. Use the fingers of your free hand to help loosen the skin at the elbow. Then cut each front foot off at the wrist joint (pictured).

CUT the head off. Remove any glands and clean out the body cavity as described in the rabbit-skinning sequence on page 27. Several long hairs usually remain on the wrists; cut these off with your knife or shears.

*How to Skin a Raccoon to Keep the Pelt Saleable*

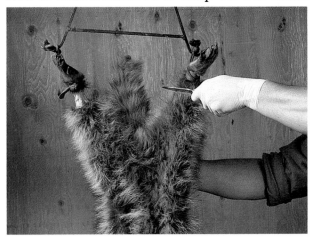

HANG the raccoon by the rear legs, and cut the skin around the rear feet. The raccoon in this picture is hanging from a special raccoon-skinning gambrel.

CUT along the inside of each rear leg to the base of the tail. Peel the pelt back to the base of the tail. Begin peeling the skin off the abdomen.

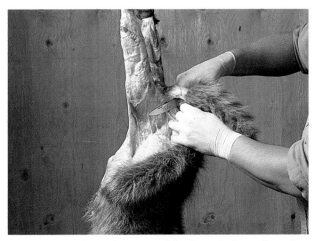

USE your knife as shown to skin the pelt from the spine above the tail. Cut through the tailbone close to the rump. Leave the tailbone inside the pelt.

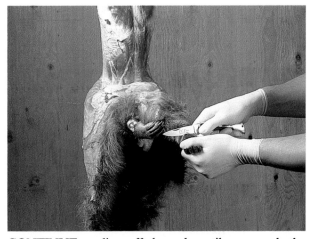

CONTINUE peeling off the pelt until you reach the shoulders, using your knife only when necessary. Cut the skin around the front feet (pictured).

PULL the pelt off the front legs and then off the head, cutting carefully at the eyes and rear base of the ears. Cut the pelt off at the nose. Turn it right-side-out to dry. Cut and peel the tail skin to remove the bone.

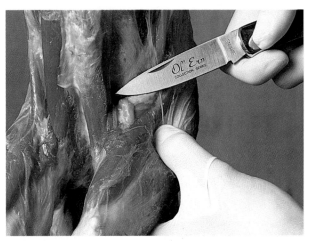

REMOVE the glands that lie under the front legs and above the base of the tail. Cut off the head and feet. Slit the abdomen from vent to neck. Remove the internal organs, rinse the raccoon, and pat it dry.

# Portioning Small Game

Small game is usually cut into serving pieces before it is cooked or frozen. Pieces are more convenient to freeze than a whole carcass, because they can be arranged into a compact bundle with few air spaces.

The portioning method shown below works with squirrels, rabbits, hares, and raccoons. The rear legs are the meatiest pieces, followed by the *saddle* or loin portion, then the front legs. The ribs contain very little meat, but can be used for making stock.

Game shears are an excellent tool for cutting up squirrels, rabbits, and hares. You may need a heavy knife, however, to cut through the thick backbone of a raccoon.

Wear rubber gloves when handling raw rabbit or hare. In some locations raccoons may carry encephalitis in early fall, so gloves are a good precaution when portioning raccoons taken at that time.

*How to Cut Up Small Game (pictured: Rabbit)*

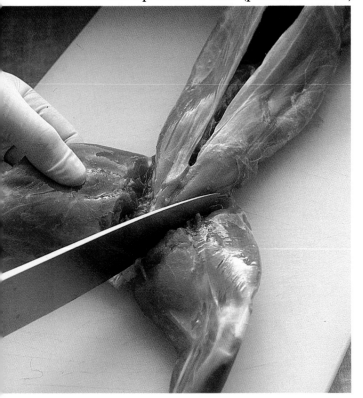

PLACE the animal on its back on a cutting board. Cut into the rear leg at a point near the backbone. When you come to the leg bone, stop cutting. If using a game shears, snip the meat around the bone.

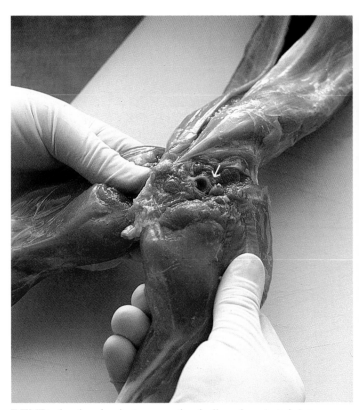

BEND the leg back to pop the ball-and-socket joint (arrow). Cut through the joint to remove the leg. Repeat with the other leg. On a large rabbit, hare, or raccoon, each rear leg can be split in two at the knee.

## A Simple Method for Cutting Up a Squirrel

CUT the squirrel in half behind the ribs (left), or along the backbone (right). If the squirrel is small, no further cutting will be necessary.

QUARTER a large squirrel by cutting each half apart. Quartered squirrels are easier to fry than halved ones, and look more attractive when served.

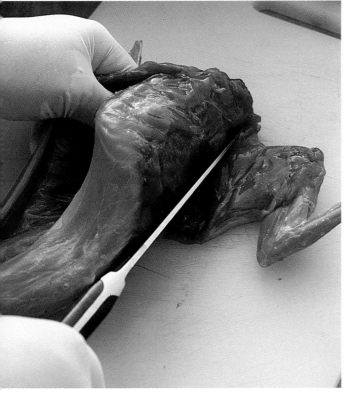

REMOVE the front legs by cutting close to the rib cage and behind the shoulder blades. The legs come off easier this way because you don't cut through joints. On a large animal, cut each leg in two at the elbow.

CUT the back into two or three pieces, depending on the animal's size. Remove the rib cage, if desired. When portioning a raccoon or large hare, you can also split the back along the spine, making four to six pieces.

# Dressing Upland Birds & Waterfowl

In warm weather, all birds should be gutted as soon as they're shot. In cool weather, gutting can wait until the end of the day's hunt.

Plucking the birds is seldom practical in the middle of a hunt. But if you do have the opportunity, you'll find the feathers pull out more easily then, while the birds are still warm. When plucking in the field, put the feathers in a bag instead of scattering them around. Be sure to check state laws on the transport of game birds. In many states, at least one wing must remain fully feathered and attached to the carcass.

When hunting in warm weather, keep a cooler filled with ice in your car or duck boat. Chill the dressed birds as soon as possible.

Before plucking or skinning any waterfowl, try to determine its age. Old birds may be tough unless cooked with moist heat. Young geese and ducks are smaller than old ones, and the plumage may not be fully colored. If you notice a lot of pinfeathers when plucking, the bird is probably young.

Most upland birds have short life spans, but turkeys and pheasants often live several years. Check the spurs on the legs of a tom turkey or rooster pheasant. Long, pointed spurs indicate an old bird; short, rounded spurs, a young one.

Birds, like big game, can be tenderized by aging. Dress the birds but leave the skin and feathers on; then store them, uncovered, in a refrigerator for a few days.

If possible, birds to be served whole should be plucked rather than skinned. The skin helps keep the meat moist. Waterfowl have thick, tough skin that doesn't tear easily, so they're easier to pluck than upland birds. An upland bird that's badly shot-up may have to be skinned, because the delicate skin would rip during plucking. Sage grouse, sea ducks, and fish-eating ducks like mergansers are usually skinned, because the skin of these birds is strongly flavored.

Skinning a bird saves time, but the meat may dry out in cooking. You can save even more time by using the breasting method shown on page 37, if you like pieces instead of a whole bird.

In rare instances, ducks have parasites in the breast meat, which show up as white, rice-like grains. Although safe to eat if thoroughly cooked, the meat is unappealing and is usually discarded.

*How to Field-dress Birds (pictured: Pheasant)*

EQUIPMENT for field-dressing upland birds and waterfowl includes (1) small hunting knife; (2) plastic bags, which can double as gloves; (3) paper towels.

CUT the skin from the vent toward the breastbone. Some hunters pluck the feathers between the vent and breastbone before cutting.

MAKE a short slit above the breast toward the chin. Pull out the windpipe. Remove the *crop,* a flexible sac that lies between the bird's breast and chin, and any undigested food it may contain.

REMOVE the entrails, including the lungs. If desired, save the heart, gizzard, and liver, storing them in a plastic bag. Be sure to trim the green gall sac from the liver. Wipe the inside of the bird with paper towels.

## How to Wet-pluck a Bird (pictured: Chukar Partridge)

WET the bird thoroughly by holding it underneath a running faucet. If wet-plucking waterfowl, rub the breast with your thumb to ensure that the thick down feathers are saturated with water.

DIP the bird several times in simmering (160° to 180°F) water. For waterfowl, add a tablespoon of dish-washing liquid to help saturate the feathers. Rinse any soapy water from the cavity of a field-dressed bird.

RUB the body feathers with your thumb. They should strip off easily. If they don't, dip the bird in hot water again. Pull out the large feathers of the wing and tail, using a pliers if necessary.

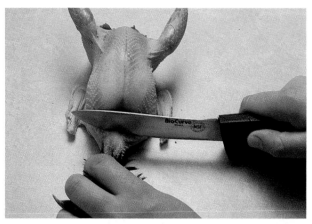

CUT off the head and tail. Slice off the feet, removing the leg tendons from upland birds (page 38) if desired. Clean the body cavity, and take out the windpipe if still present. Rinse the cavity, and pat the bird dry.

## How to Dry-pluck a Bird (pictured: Bobwhite Quail)

GRASP only a few feathers at a time, and pull gently in the direction in which they grow. Pluck over a grocery bag to minimize the mess.

USE a pliers, if necessary, to pull out the wing and tail feathers. Some hunters cut off the outer two joints of the wings; little meat is lost.

SINGE any downy feathers or "hair" with a gas burner. Finish cleaning as described in the last step of the wet-plucking sequence shown above.

*How to Wax Waterfowl (pictured: Mallard)*

HEAT a large pot of water to a gentle boil. Melt several chunks of special duck-picking wax or paraffin in the water. The floating layer of melted wax should be at least ¼ inch thick.

ROUGH-PLUCK the larger feathers from the body, legs, wings, and tail. Pull only a few feathers at a time. Leave the smaller feathers on the bird, since they make the wax adhere better.

DIP the bird in the wax and water. Swish it around gently, then slowly remove it from the wax. Hold the bird up until the wax hardens enough that you can set it down on newspapers without sticking. Or, hang it by wedging the head between closely spaced nails on a board.

ALLOW the bird to cool until the wax is fairly hard. To speed the process, you can dip the bird in a bucket of cold water. Repeat the dipping and cooling until a layer of wax has built up at least ⅛ inch thick. Allow the wax to cool completely and harden.

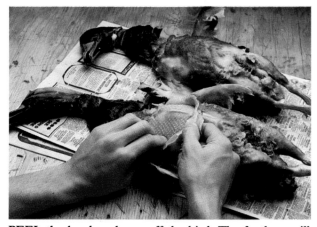

PEEL the hardened wax off the bird. The feathers will come off with the wax, leaving the skin smooth. You can reuse the wax if you melt it again and strain it through cheesecloth to remove the feathers.

CUT off the head, feet, and tail. Remove the windpipe and entrails if the bird was not dressed before waxing. Remove wax from the cavity of a dressed bird. Clean the cavity thoroughly, rinse the bird, and pat it dry.

*How to Skin a Bird (pictured: Pheasant)*

CUT off the last two joints of the wing with game shears or a knife. Cut off the feet, removing the leg tendons from an upland bird (page 38) if desired.

PLACE fingers in the slit where the crop was removed during field-dressing; pull to skin breast and legs. If crop is still in, slit skin and remove crop first.

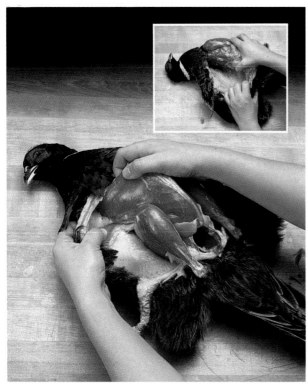

PULL the skin away from the wing joints, turning the skin inside-out over the joints as though peeling off a stocking. Free both wings, then peel the skin off the back of the bird (inset).

REMOVE the head and tail with game shears. If the bird wasn't dressed before skinning, pull out the windpipe and entrails. Clean the cavity thoroughly. Rinse the bird and pat it dry.

*How to Breast a Bird to Retain the Legs (pictured: Pheasant)*

CUT off the feet and pull the skin off the breast and legs as described in the skinning sequence on the opposite page. Do not skin the wings.

SLICE breast halves away from the breastbone, using a fillet knife. Keep the blade as close to the bone as possible. Cut the meat away from the wishbone to free completely.

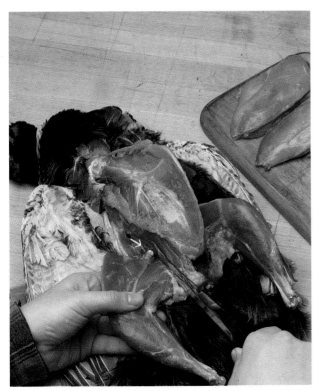

PUSH the leg down, popping the ball-and-socket joint (arrow). Cut through the joint to remove the leg. Remove other leg. If the bird wasn't field-dressed, remove liver, heart, and gizzard if you wish to save them.

CUT apart the thigh and drumstick if desired. Dispose of the carcass. With this method of breasting, the only meat discarded is on the back and wings. The boneless breast halves are easy to cook.

## *How to Remove Leg Tendons from Upland Birds*

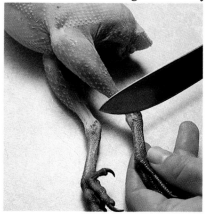 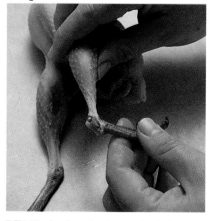 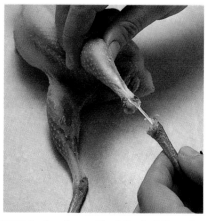

CUT the skin around the bottom of the drumstick, either before or after plucking. Do not cut deeply, or you will sever the tendons.

BEND the foot back and forth four or five times. This helps loosen the tendons, which connect the foot to the muscles in the leg.

PULL the foot off while holding the leg with your other hand. The legs are easier to eat if the tough tendons have been removed.

## *Tips for Dressing Upland Birds and Waterfowl*

MAKE a large cut when field-dressing a turkey (pictured) or large sage grouse so you can get your whole hand inside the body cavity (left). This makes it easier to take out the entrails (right).

REMOVE entrails with a special bird-gutting knife. Insert the hook into the body, then rotate the knife and pull it out. The entrails will twist around the hook. A small forked stick can be used the same way.

PLUCK waterfowl by using a rubber-fingered "power picker." Many shooting preserves, and some resorts near good waterfowl areas, will power-pick your ducks or geese for a small fee.

BONE the thigh of a pheasant (pictured) or other bird to make a boneless fillet. Fold the thigh in half so the bone is on top. Slip your knife or shears under the end of the bone, and cut the meat away.

# Portioning Upland Birds & Waterfowl

Whether to portion a bird, and how, depends mainly on its size and the cooking method. Any upland bird or waterfowl can be cooked whole. The larger ones, such as pheasant, turkey, mallard, and goose, can be cut into traditional pieces if preferred. Birds up to the size of a pheasant can also be split into halves.

If you portion a bird, skinning is optional. When you cut it up, save the backbone, neck, and any bones left from breasting. These parts make excellent stock (page 145). Most cooks do not make stock from small birds like doves, woodcock, and quail.

Breasting is quick and easy, and many hunters prefer it when they have a number of birds to process. The breasting method shown on page 37 saves not only the breast but also the thighs and drumsticks, so very little meat is wasted.

*How to Split a Bird into Halves (pictured: Hungarian Partridge)*

SPLIT the back by cutting along one side of the backbone with game shears. If desired, cut along the other side of the backbone and remove it.

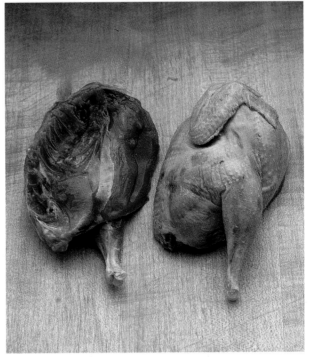

CUT along one side of the breastbone and through the wishbone. You can remove the breastbone by making a second cut along the other side of it.

*How to Cut Up a Bird (pictured: Pheasant)*

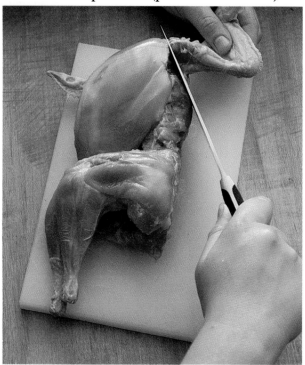

REMOVE the wings by cutting through the joint next to the breast. For another way of handling the wings, see the photo sequence of the French portioning technique on the opposite page.

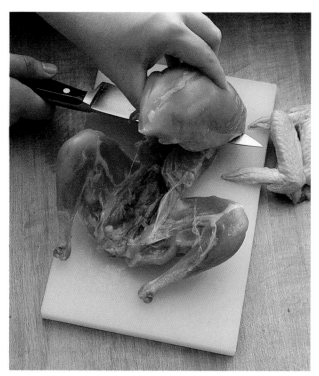

SEPARATE the breast from the back by cutting through the ribs. When you reach the shoulder, grasp the breast in one hand and the back in the other; bend the carcass as if it were hinged. Cut the breast and back apart.

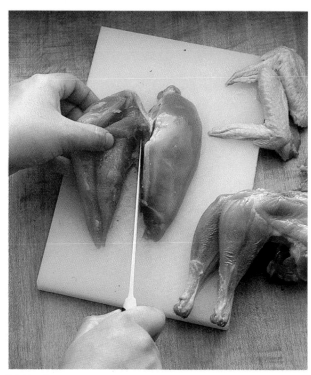

DIVIDE the breast into halves by cutting along one side of the breastbone, then cutting away the wishbone. You can also cut along the other side of the breastbone and remove it. Or, bone the breast as shown in the breasting sequence on page 37.

BEGIN cutting the leg away from the backbone, then bend it back to expose the ball-and-socket joint (arrow). Cut through the socket to remove the leg. If desired, separate the thigh from the drumstick by cutting through the knee joint.

*How to Cut Up a Bird Using the French Technique (pictured: Pheasant)*

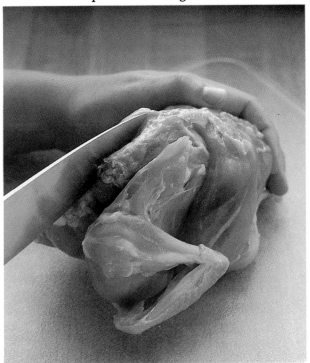

LOCATE the shoulder blade, where the wing is attached to the back of the bird. Slice between the shoulder blade and backbone, sliding the knife next to the ribs. Do not cut the wing completely off.

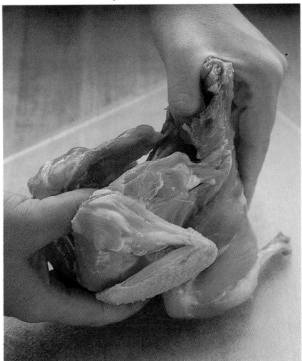

GRASP the breastbone in one hand and the backbone in the other. Then pull as pictured, separating the breast portion from the back portion. The legs will remain attached to the backbone.

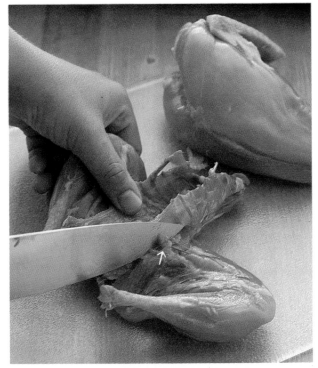

BEGIN cutting the leg away from the backbone, then bend it back to expose the ball-and-socket joint (arrow). Cut through the socket to remove the leg. If desired, separate the thigh from the drumstick by cutting through the knee joint.

SPLIT the breast lengthwise, then cut each half as shown. This technique leaves some breast meat attached to the wings, so the serving portions are more nearly even. The added meat from the breast is especially desirable if you haven't saved the last two wing joints.

# Birds & Small Game: Final Cleaning Steps

A quick rinse before cooking or freezing is often all that is necessary for the final cleaning step. But a little extra effort will often improve the quality of your meat.

Examine birds and small game carefully, looking for shot and for any fur or feathers the shot may have driven in. Pick all these out with fine tweezers, the point of a sharp knife, or a fly-tying forceps.

Soak the meat only if it is badly shot up and saturated with blood. Then, immerse it for an hour or two in milk, or in a solution of 2 quarts water to 1 tablespoon baking soda. If the meat has been cut into portions, soak only the damaged ones. Rinse the meat well after soaking.

Remove all fat from a raccoon before cooking or freezing. The fat is strong-tasting and oily, and gives the meat an undesirable flavor. Rabbits, hares, and squirrels have little if any fat.

Rinse the hearts and livers to remove any clotted blood. If the top of the heart is ragged, trim it off. The bile sac should have been removed from the liver during field dressing. Cut away any part of the liver or meat that has a green bile stain.

Most hunters save turkey gizzards, and some save pheasant and waterfowl gizzards. Clean them as shown in the photo sequence on the opposite page. Gizzards can be fried whole, chopped and mixed into stuffing, or added to the stockpot.

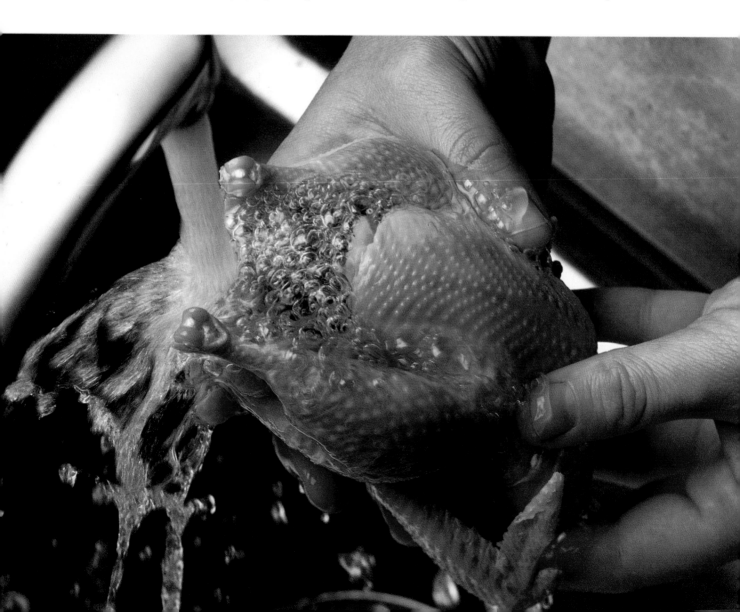

## How to Clean a Gizzard

SPLIT the gizzard between the two lobes, and clean out all food matter and grit. Do not put the contents down a kitchen garbage disposal, since they include small rocks that cannot be ground up.

SET the opened gizzard on your cutting board, with the tough inside membrane facing down. Skin the meat from the membrane with a fillet knife. Discard this membrane. The outside membrane can be left on, if desired.

## Tips for Final Cleaning

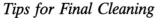

HOLD a piece of upland bird or small game up to a light. The meat is somewhat translucent, so you may be able to see shot (arrows) embedded in it.

USE a game shears to remove fat from a raccoon. Cut down into the fat until some meat is exposed, then snip between the fat and the meat.

# Freezing Wild Game

Many hunters spend hours dressing and portioning their game, then hurriedly wrap it in a plastic bag and toss it in the freezer. When they defrost it, they're surprised to find their efforts were wasted, because the meat is dried out, or *freezer burned.*

To prevent freezer burn, double-wrap the meat or freeze it in water. This step is especially important if you own a modern frost-free freezer. In a freezer of this type, a fan unit pulls the moisture out of the air to prevent frost build-up. Unfortunately, it also pulls the moisture out of poorly wrapped meat.

Remove all fat from big game and raccoons before wrapping them for the freezer. The fat of these animals may turn rancid even while frozen, affecting the taste of the meat.

Backstraps, sirloin tips, and other choice boneless cuts of big game should not be steaked before freezing. Moisture escapes from each cut surface, so smaller pieces lose more moisture than bigger ones. Freeze the whole cut, or divide it into two or three pieces large enough for a family meal. This way, you can use a piece as a roast, or steak it after thawing.

The same principle applies to freezing stew, burger, or sausage meat. Freeze larger chunks, then cut them to size or grind them just before cooking. Game ground with fat for burger meat does not keep as long as plain ground meat, because the fat can turn rancid.

Mark all packages clearly with waterproof, permanent ink. Note the species of animal, the type of cut if applicable, the weight or number of servings, and the date. An old, potentially tough animal should be indicated as such. Some hunters mark with a different color of ink each season, so they can tell at a glance which packages are oldest.

To promote rapid freezing, arrange the wrapped packages in a single layer in the freezer, then turn the freezer to the coldest setting. Stack the packages only after they're frozen.

Thaw frozen game by placing the wrapped package on a plate in the refrigerator at least a full day before you want to cook the meat. The cool temperature minimizes bacterial growth, and the slow thaw helps tenderize the meat.

*Freezer Storage Chart*

| TYPE OF MEAT | WRAPPING METHOD* | MAXIMUM STORAGE TIME |
|---|---|---|
| Big Game Roasts | Standard butcher wrap | 10 months |
| Big Game Steaks | Standard butcher wrap | 8 months |
| Big Game Ribs | Foil wrap | 5 months |
| Big Game Organs | Standard butcher wrap<br>Water pack | 4 months<br>6 months |
| Big Game Chunks | Freezer bag and paper | 6 months |
| Big Game Burger | Freezer bag and paper | 4 months |
| Cut-up Small Game | Standard butcher wrap<br>Water pack | 8 months<br>1 year |
| Small Game Organs | Water pack | 10 months |
| Whole Large Birds | Foil wrap | 5 months |
| Whole Small Birds | Standard butcher wrap<br>Water pack | 6 months<br>1 year |
| Cut-up Upland Birds | Standard butcher wrap<br>Water pack | 8 months<br>1 year |
| Cut-up Waterfowl | Standard butcher wrap<br>Water pack | 8 months<br>1 year |
| Bird Giblets | Water pack | 4 months |
| Game Stock | Freezer containers | 4 months |

*Photo instructions given for all wrapping techniques on pages 46-49.

## The Standard Butcher Wrap

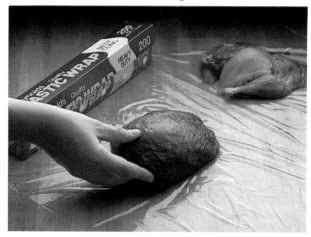

PLACE the meat on the center of a large piece of plastic wrap. If wrapping a cut-up bird or small-game animal, arrange the pieces to form a compact bundle, with as little space between them as possible.

BRING one end of the wrap over the meat, then fold both sides over it. Gently squeeze out as much air as possible. Bring the other end over, or roll the bundle to it, continuing to squeeze out air.

LAY the plastic-wrapped bundle on a corner of a large piece of heavy-duty freezer paper (shiny side up).

ROLL the bundle once, so both the top and bottom are covered with a single layer of freezer paper.

FOLD one side of the freezer paper over the bundle. Tuck in any loose edges of the paper.

ROLL the bundle again. Fold the other side of the freezer paper over the bundle, tucking the corner neatly.

FASTEN the end with freezer tape when wrapping is complete. Tape the seam also, if desired.

LABEL with a waterproof pen. Note the species, cut, quantity, date, and maturity of animal if noted.

## The Foil Wrap

USE foil instead of plastic wrap for ribs or other odd-shaped cuts. Place the meat on a large piece of heavy-duty aluminum foil.

PRESS the foil around the meat to eliminate air spaces. Be careful not to puncture the foil with the bones. Use two pieces of foil if necessary.

BUTCHER-WRAP with freezer paper, eliminating as much air as possible. Seal all seams with freezer tape, and label the package.

## How to Wrap a Whole Large Game Bird

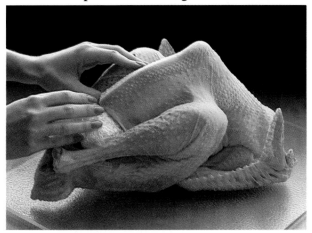

STUFF wadded plastic wrap into the body cavity. This reduces the chance of freezer burn.

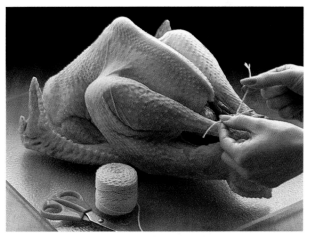

TIE the drumsticks together with kitchen string. They'll stick out less, and wrapping will be easier.

WRAP the bird with heavy-duty aluminum foil. You may need several pieces to cover the entire bird. Press the foil snugly around the body.

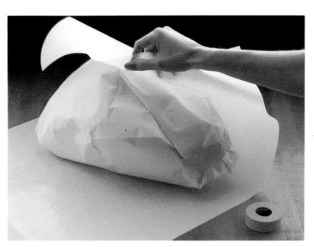

COMPLETE the wrapping with a double layer of heavy-duty freezer paper. Seal all the seams with freezer tape, and label the package.

47

## How to Water-pack Game in Containers

SAVE waxed dairy cartons. Open up the tops, and wash the cartons well. Or, use plastic freezer containers. Square-bottomed containers make the best use of your freezer space.

PLACE game in cartons or plastic containers. Use pint- or quart-sized cartons for small whole birds, half-gallon cartons for large ones. Tiny birds like woodcock or doves can be frozen four to six per carton. Layer giblets in a small carton. Arrange cut-up birds or small game in a plastic container. Cover the game with water, jiggle it to eliminate air bubbles, and freeze.

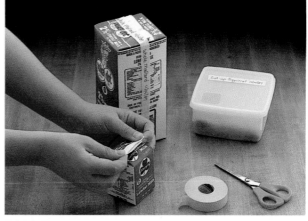

CHECK after the water is frozen to be sure the game is completely covered with a layer of ice. If not, add cold water and refreeze.

FOLD the top of a dairy carton closed, if possible. Wrap a band of freezer tape around the carton so it sticks to itself; label the tape. Label the lid of a plastic container.

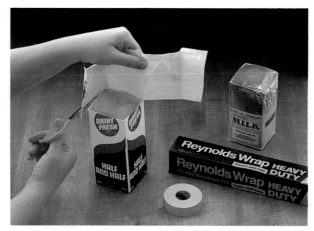

CUT off the top if the carton can't be closed, or if it isn't filled to the fold with ice. Trim at the ice level. Cover the top with heavy-duty aluminum foil. Wrap freezer tape around the edge of the foil, and label it.

ADD more giblets to the frozen ones as you shoot more birds. Place fresh giblets on top of the frozen ones. Add cold water; refreeze. Keep track of the number of giblets on a piece of tape, until you have enough for a meal.

## How to Water-pack Cut-up Game in a Plastic Bag

PLACE a zip-lock plastic freezer bag in a cake pan, then arrange the pieces in the bag. The bag should lie on its side in the pan.

ADD water to completely cover the pieces of game. Squeeze out all the air, and seal the top of the bag. Set the pan in the freezer.

BUTCHER-WRAP the frozen bag with freezer paper. This keeps it from ripping or puncturing, which could open the meat to freezer burn.

## Tips for Freezing Game

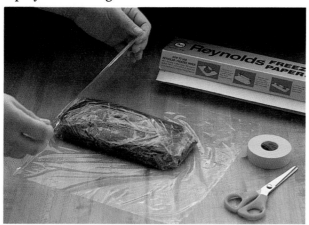

TRIPLE-WRAP cut steaks or chops for additional protection from freezer burn. Use two layers of plastic wrap, then finish with a layer of freezer paper.

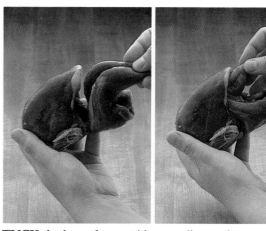

TUCK the legs of a partridge, quail, or other small bird into the body cavity before wrapping. The package will be more compact, with less air inside to dry the meat.

PUT stew chunks or ground meat in a zip-lock plastic freezer bag. To push out air, immerse the bag almost to its top in a sinkful of cold water. Seal the bag while it's still in the water. Wrap it in freezer paper.

FREEZE 1-cup batches of cooked game stock in small dairy cartons or plastic freezer containers. When a recipe calls for stock, take a carton from the freezer, hold it under warm water, then slide the frozen stock out.

49

# Cooking Big Game

Big-game meat, if cooked properly, is even tastier than choice beef. And because it's leaner than beef, it also has fewer calories. But the lean meat can become tough and dry if cooked incorrectly.

To make sure big-game meat doesn't dry out, cook it with moist heat or keep it on the rare side. One exception is bear meat. Always cook it thoroughly, like pork, because bears may carry trichinosis.

The external fat of big game is strong-tasting and tallowy, so remove it before cooking. To tenderize tough cuts, marinate them in a mixture of oil and wine (page 148), or in a packaged beef marinade.

Most recipes for deer work equally well for antelope, elk, and moose. Generally, antelope and elk meat is finer-grained than deer and moose. Of the antlered animals, elk probably tastes most like beef;

antelope, least like it. Bear meat is stronger, darker, and coarser than other big game, and is usually prepared with more seasoning.

How good the meat tastes, however, depends less on the species of the animal than on its sex and age, the time of year it was killed, and the care you take with it after the kill. A buck taken during the rut, for instance, is usually stronger-tasting and tougher than one taken earlier in the season.

The animal's diet also affects the flavor. A corn-fed deer is much tastier than one forced to eat low-nutrition foods like red cedar. If you store meat from several animals in your freezer and notice that meat from one tastes particularly strong, mark all the other packages from that animal. Then you can prepare it in a way that minimizes the flavor.

## Tips for Preparing Big Game Meat

REMOVE silverskin with a fillet knife. Cut into one end of the meat to the silverskin. Turn blade parallel to silverskin. Hold silverskin firmly with fingertips, and push knife away from them as though skinning a fish fillet. Very little meat is removed with the silverskin this way.

BUTTERFLY small-diameter backstraps or tenderloins to make larger steaks. Cut a steak twice as thick as you want. Then slice it into two "wings" of equal thickness; leave the two wings joined by an edge of meat. Open steak up, and flatten slightly.

CUT *across* the grain of the meat when steaking it or making slices for sautéeing. Cut *with* the grain, however, when making slices for jerky. Partially frozen meat is easiest to slice.

CHOP or grind trimmed big-game scrap with 15 to 20% beef fat to make burger. Use a food processor or meat grinder; the blades must be sharp. Fat is easiest to chop if kept very cold.

## Roasting Big Game

There are two basic ways to roast big game: with dry heat and moist heat. Dry-heat roasting includes high- and low-temperature methods. The most common method of moist-heat roasting is braising, which includes pot roasting.

Only prime roasts are candidates for dry-heat, high-temperature cooking. These include the top round, sirloin tip, backstrap, and rump roasts. The tenderloin of a moose, elk, or large deer may also be used. These prime cuts are naturally tender, and do not need long, slow cooking for tenderizing.

For high-temperature cooking, select a roast between 2 and 5 inches thick, or a thinner piece you can roll and tie (page 25). First, brown the meat in hot fat, then roast it in a hot (400° to 450°) oven. With these high temperatures, roasts should be cooked only rare to medium. If cooked well-done, they dry out and shrink.

Low-temperature roasting is another option for these same prime cuts. And it's necessary for such medium-tender cuts as the bottom round and eye of round, which need longer cooking to ensure tenderness. Cover the meat with bacon or a sheet of beef or pork fat (available from your butcher), or baste it frequently. Cook it in a slow (300° to 325°) oven. With low heat, roasts may be cooked rare, medium, or well-done.

When roasting with dry heat, use a meat thermometer to check for doneness. The chart below gives temperatures for various stages of doneness. Remove the meat from the oven when it reads 5° below the ideal temperature; it will continue to heat on the platter. It will slice better if you wait 10 to 15 minutes before carving.

Moist heat tenderizes shoulder roasts and other tough cuts, and also works well with the bottom round and eye of round. Brown the roast in hot fat, then add liquid and flavoring and cover the pan tightly. Cook the meat until tender, on the stove top or in a moderate (325° to 350°) oven. When pot-roasting, add vegetables during the last hour or so of cooking. Braised meat is always served well-done.

### Internal Temperature of Meat at Various Degrees of Doneness

| DEGREE OF DONENESS | INTERNAL TEMPERATURE |
|---|---|
| Rare | 130° to 135° |
| Medium-rare | 135° to 140° |
| Medium | 140° to 145° |
| Medium-well | 150° to 155° |
| Well-done | 155° to 160° |

### Roast Boneless Sirloin Tip ◆ LOW-FAT

*You may substitute a backstrap, rolled top round, or rump roast for the sirloin tip in this high-temperature method. Sirloin tip roasts from elk or moose may be too large to roast with this method.*

1 boneless deer or antelope sirloin tip roast or other suitable roast, 2 to 5 inches thick
1 to 2 tablespoons olive oil or vegetable oil

2 to 4 servings per pound

Heat oven to 450°. In medium skillet or Dutch oven, sear roast well on all sides in oil over medium-high heat. Place on rack in roasting pan. Roast to desired doneness (see chart at bottom left), 18 to 28 minutes per pound; remove roast when temperature is 5° less than desired. Allow meat to rest for 10 to 15 minutes before carving.

## Roast Big Game Tenderloin ▸ LOW-FAT

*In this combination of high- and low-temperature roasting, a whole tenderloin is seared in the oven, then roasted at a reduced temperature. You may substitute the loin from an antelope or deer.*

1 whole elk, moose, or large deer tenderloin, 1½ to 3½ pounds
   Peanut or vegetable oil
   Salt and freshly ground black pepper
1 recipe Madeira Game Sauce (page 147), optional

2 to 4 servings per pound

Heat oven to 450°. Place tenderloin in roasting pan; tuck small end under. Brush tenderloin with oil. Roast at 450° for 10 minutes. Reduce heat to 350°. Roast to desired doneness (see chart on opposite page), 20 to 25 minutes per pound; remove roast when temperature is 5° less than desired. Allow meat to rest for 10 minutes before carving. Sprinkle with salt and pepper. Serve with Madeira Game Sauce.

## Peppered Antelope Roast ↑

*This recipe uses the low-temperature roasting method. Substitute a deer or small elk sirloin tip; deer, elk, or moose backstrap or rump roast; or antelope or deer bottom round.*

2 medium cloves garlic
1 boneless rolled antelope or deer top round roast or other suitable roast, 3 to 5 pounds
   Vegetable oil
   Cracked black pepper
8 to 10 slices bacon

2 to 4 servings per pound

Heat oven to 325°. Cut each garlic clove into 4 or 5 slivers. Make 8 or 10 shallow slits in roast. Insert a garlic sliver into each slit. Place roast on rack in roasting pan; brush with oil. Sprinkle pepper liberally over roast. Cover roast with bacon slices. Roast to desired doneness (see chart on opposite page), 22 to 32 minutes per pound; remove roast when temperature is 5° less than desired. Allow meat to rest for 10 to 15 minutes before carving. Serve with pan juices.

## Big Game Pot Roast ↑

*Use the shoulder roast, rump roast, or bottom round from any big game for this classic pot roast. If you've had a butcher cut up your animal, you will have some packages marked "chuck," which are perfect for pot roasting.*

⅓ cup all-purpose flour
1 teaspoon dried basil leaves
½ teaspoon dried marjoram leaves
½ teaspoon dried thyme leaves
½ teaspoon salt
¼ teaspoon pepper
2½ to 3-pound deer, antelope, elk, moose, or
    bear roast
3 tablespoons vegetable oil
1 can (10½ ounces) condensed French
    onion soup
½ cup water, broth, or wine
1 bay leaf
1 rutabaga, peeled and cut into 1-inch cubes
4 to 6 medium carrots, cut into 2-inch pieces
3 stalks celery, cut into 2-inch pieces

4 to 6 servings

Heat oven to 350°. In large plastic food-storage bag, combine flour, basil, marjoram, thyme, salt, and pepper; shake to mix. Add meat; shake to coat. In Dutch oven, brown meat on both sides in oil. Add remaining flour mixture, soup, water, and bay leaf. Heat to boiling. Remove from heat; cover. Bake for 1½ hours. Add rutabaga, carrots, and celery. Re-cover. Bake until meat and vegetables are tender, 1 to 1½ hours longer. Discard bay leaf before serving.

## Grilled Antelope Shoulder

*When cutting up an antelope or small deer, leave one front quarter whole from shoulder to shank. Tenderize the meat with a marinade, then grill for an outdoor party.*

MARINADE:
1½ cups vegetable oil
½ cup red wine vinegar
1 small onion, chopped
2 cloves garlic, minced
1 teaspoon cracked black pepper
½ teaspoon dry mustard
½ teaspoon salt

1 antelope front quarter

4 to 8 servings

In small saucepan, combine all marinade ingredients. Heat until very hot but not boiling. Cool slightly. Place antelope quarter in large oven cooking bag or baking dish. Add marinade. Seal bag or cover dish. Marinate in refrigerator for 2 to 3 days, turning meat over several times.

Start charcoal briquets in grill. When briquets are covered with ash, spread them evenly in grill. Place grate above hot coals. Place antelope quarter on grate. Grill until desired doneness, 40 to 55 minutes, turning meat over once and basting with marinade.

## Rolled Stuffed Roast of Venison

*Use a top or bottom round roast for this method. The meat should be no more than one inch thick; butterfly (page 25) if necessary. If using elk or moose, you may have to cut the roast into two halves, and freeze one half for later.*

6 slices bacon
1 medium onion, chopped
½ cup chopped celery
½ cup chopped carrot
⅓ cup seasoned dry bread crumbs
2 teaspoons dried parsley flakes
¼ teaspoon salt
⅛ teaspoon pepper
3 to 4-pound boneless deer, antelope, elk, or
    moose roast, up to 1 inch thick
3 slices bacon, cut in half

6 to 8 servings

### *How to Prepare Rolled Stuffed Roast of Venison*

FRY 6 slices bacon in large skillet over medium heat until crisp. Remove from heat. Transfer bacon to paper towels to drain. Reserve 3 tablespoons bacon fat. Crumble drained bacon; set aside. Heat oven to 325°.

COOK and stir onion, celery, and carrot in reserved bacon fat over medium heat until tender. Remove from heat. Stir in crumbled bacon, bread crumbs, parsley flakes, salt, and pepper.

SPREAD vegetable mixture evenly on roast. Pat vegetable mixture firmly into place. Roll up jelly-roll style, rolling with the grain of the meat.

TIE roast with kitchen string (page 25). Place in roasting pan. Top roast with 3 halved slices bacon. Roast to desired doneness (page 54), 22 to 30 minutes per pound.

57

## Venison Roast Burgundy

2 tablespoons all-purpose flour
1 cup burgundy
½ teaspoon dried rosemary leaves
½ teaspoon dried marjoram leaves
½ teaspoon salt
¼ teaspoon pepper
3 to 4-pound deer, elk, or moose roast
4 carrots, cut into 2-inch pieces
2 medium onions, quartered
2 bay leaves
1 tablespoon cornstarch
¼ cup cold water
½ teaspoon brown bouquet sauce, optional

6 to 8 servings

Heat oven to 350°. Add flour to large (14 × 20-inch) oven cooking bag; shake to distribute. Place bag in roasting pan. Pour wine into bag; stir with plastic or wooden spoon to blend into flour. Set aside.

In small mixing bowl, mix rosemary, marjoram, salt, and pepper. Rub herb mixture evenly over meat. Place meat in cooking bag with flour. Add carrots, onions, and bay leaves to cooking bag. Close bag with provided nylon tie. Make six ½-inch slits in top of bag. Roast until meat is tender, 1½ to 2½ hours. Remove meat to heated platter. With slotted spoon, transfer vegetables to platter. Keep warm. Discard bay leaves. Pour juices into small saucepan. In 1-cup measure, blend cornstarch into water. Stir half of cornstarch mixture into juices. Heat to boiling, stirring constantly. Cook, stirring constantly, until thickened and bubbly. Blend in additional cornstarch if thicker gravy is desired; cook and stir until thickened and bubbly. Stir in bouquet sauce. Serve gravy with meat and vegetables.

## Big Game Belgium

*Slow braising tenderizes the shoulder roast in this recipe. You may substitute any big-game roast for the elk shoulder. Serve roast with buttered noodles.*

½ cup all-purpose flour
2 teaspoons dried thyme leaves
¼ teaspoon salt
½ teaspoon pepper
3 pound elk shoulder roast, about 2 inches thick
3 tablespoons olive oil or vegetable oil
½ pound salt pork, diced
3 tablespoons butter or margarine
3 medium onions, thinly sliced
1 tablespoon granulated sugar
1 bottle (12 ounces) dark beer
2 tablespoons packed brown sugar
1 tablespoon snipped fresh parsley

4 to 6 servings

Heat oven to 325°. In large plastic food-storage bag, combine flour, thyme, salt, and pepper; shake to mix. Add meat; shake to coat. In Dutch oven, brown meat in oil over medium heat. Remove meat; set aside. Add salt pork to Dutch oven. Cook over medium heat, stirring frequently, until salt pork is crisp and golden brown. With slotted spoon, transfer salt pork to small mixing bowl; set aside. Melt butter in Dutch oven. Add onions. Cook and stir over medium heat until tender. Add granulated sugar. Cook and stir until onions are brown, about 10 minutes. Add beer and brown sugar. Stir, scraping bottom of pan to loosen browned bits. Return meat to Dutch oven. Add reserved salt pork. Cover; bake until meat is tender, about 2 hours. Transfer meat to platter. Garnish with parsley. Serve with pan juices if desired.

## Venison Sauerbraten ◆ LOW-FAT

*Marinating tenderizes and adds flavor to this roast. Use a shoulder roast, bottom round, or rump roast. Serve with hot buttered noodles and sliced apples.*

MARINADE:
  6 cups water
  1 large onion, sliced
  2 teaspoons salt
 10 whole black peppercorns
 10 whole juniper berries, optional
  6 whole cloves
  1 bay leaf
 ½ cup vinegar

3½ to 4-pound deer, elk, or moose roast
  2 tablespoons vegetable oil
  1 medium red or green cabbage (about 2½ pounds), cut into 8 wedges
 15 gingersnaps, finely crushed
  2 teaspoons sugar

6 to 8 servings

In large saucepan, combine all marinade ingredients except vinegar. Heat to boiling. Add vinegar. Cool slightly. Place roast in large glass or ceramic mixing bowl. Pour cooled marinade over roast. Cover tightly with plastic wrap. Refrigerate 2 to 3 days, turning meat once or twice.

Remove roast from marinade, reserving marinade. In Dutch oven, brown roast on all sides in oil over medium heat. Add marinade. Reduce heat; cover. Cook over low heat until tender, 2 to 3 hours. Heat oven to 175° just before meat is tender. With slotted spoon, transfer roast to oven-proof serving platter. Keep warm in oven.

Strain cooking liquid into 2-quart measure. Add water if necessary to equal 5 cups. Return liquid to Dutch oven. Heat to boiling. Add cabbage wedges. Return to boiling. Reduce heat; cover. Simmer until cabbage is tender, 15 to 20 minutes. With slotted spoon, transfer cabbage to platter with meat. In small bowl, combine crushed gingersnaps and sugar. Stir into liquid in Dutch oven. Cook over low heat, stirring occasionally, until bubbly and slightly thickened. Serve gingersnap sauce with roast and cabbage wedges.

## ← Big Game Baked Round Steak

*This is a good "company" dish. Once the meat is in the oven, you are free to enjoy your guests. The finished steaks are very attractive, with a slightly barbecued appearance.*

2 to 3 pounds boneless deer, antelope, elk, or
    moose round steak, 1 inch thick
½ cup all-purpose flour
2 teaspoons salt
¼ teaspoon pepper
1 to 2 tablespoons butter or margarine
2 to 3 tablespoons olive oil or vegetable oil
3 tablespoons finely chopped onion
    Brown sugar
    Catsup
    Dried basil leaves
1 tablespoon butter or margarine, cut up
¼ cup venison stock (page 144) or beef broth

6 to 8 servings

Heat oven to 350°. Trim meat; cut into serving-sized pieces. Pound to ½-inch thickness with meat mallet. On a sheet of waxed paper, mix flour, salt, and pepper. Dip steaks in flour mixture, turning to coat. In large skillet, melt 1 tablespoon butter in 2 table-spoons oil over medium-high heat. Add coated steaks; brown on both sides. Fry in two batches if necessary, adding additional butter and oil. Arrange browned steaks in 12×8-inch baking pan. Sprinkle with onion. Top each steak with 1 teaspoon packed brown sugar and 1 teaspoon catsup. Sprinkle lightly with basil. Dot with 1 tablespoon butter. Add stock to drippings in skillet. Cook over medium heat for about 1 minute, stirring to loosen any browned bits. Add to baking pan. Cover with aluminum foil. Bake for about 45 minutes. Remove foil. If meat appears dry, add a small amount of stock or water to pan. Bake until browned on top, about 15 minutes longer.

## Fillet of Venison

*You may substitute a moose or elk tenderloin, or the loin portion of the backstrap from an antelope or deer, for the deer tenderloin in this recipe.*

1 whole deer tenderloin, 1 to 3 pounds
1 to 2 tablespoons butter or margarine
1 tablespoon olive oil or vegetable oil
    Salt and freshly ground black pepper
    Madeira Game Sauce (page 147), optional

2 or 3 servings per pound

Remove all surface fat and silverskin from tender-loin. Slice across grain into 1-inch-thick fillets. In medium skillet, melt butter in oil over medium-low heat. Add fillets; cook to desired doneness over medium-high heat, turning once. Salt and pepper to taste. Serve with Madeira Game Sauce.

## Grilled Loin with Brown Sugar Baste  → 

*Thick big-game steaks are also excellent in this recipe.*

2 to 4 pounds deer, antelope, elk, or moose loin portion or whole backstrap
3 tablespoons butter or margarine
3 tablespoons soy sauce
3 tablespoons packed brown sugar

2 or 3 servings per pound

Start charcoal briquets in grill. Remove all fat and silverskin from meat. Cut into lengths about 4 inches long, or about 6 to 8 ounces each. In small saucepan, melt butter over medium heat. Add soy sauce and brown sugar. Cook, stirring constantly, until brown sugar dissolves and sauce bubbles.

When charcoal briquets are covered with ash, spread them evenly in grill. Place grate above hot coals. Place meat on grate. Grill on one side until seared. Turn meat over; brush with brown sugar mixture. Continue grilling, brushing frequently with brown sugar mixture and turning occasionally to grill all sides, until desired doneness.

## Big Game Swiss Steak

*Any big-game steak can be used with this method. The long, slow cooking tenderizes even tough cuts.*

1½ pounds boneless deer round steak or other big-game steak, ½ to 1 inch thick
⅓ cup all-purpose flour
1 teaspoon salt
¼ teaspoon pepper
3 to 4 tablespoons bacon fat
1 can (16 ounces) stewed tomatoes
¾ cup water
1 teaspoon instant beef bouillon granules
½ teaspoon dried basil leaves
½ teaspoon dried marjoram leaves
1 medium onion, thinly sliced

4 to 6 servings

Trim meat; cut into serving-sized pieces. Pound to ¼- to ½-inch thickness with meat mallet. On a sheet of waxed paper, mix flour, salt, and pepper. Dip steaks in flour mixture, turning to coat. In large skillet, heat bacon fat over medium heat. Add coated steaks; brown lightly on both sides. Fry in two batches if necessary. In small mixing bowl, mix stewed tomatoes, water, bouillon granules, basil, and marjoram; pour over steaks. Top meat and tomatoes with sliced onion. Heat to boiling. Reduce heat; cover. Simmer over very low heat until meat is tender, 1½ to 2 hours. Skim fat if desired.

## Bear Steak Flamade

*This hearty dish is good after outdoor winter activities. Serve with mashed potatoes, homemade wheat bread, and colorful vegetables.*

⅓ cup all-purpose flour
1 teaspoon salt
¼ teaspoon pepper
2 pounds bear round steak, 1 inch thick
½ cup butter or margarine, divided
2 tablespoons olive oil or vegetable oil
4 medium onions, thinly sliced
1½ cups beer
¼ teaspoon dried marjoram leaves
¼ teaspoon dried thyme leaves
1 bay leaf

6 to 8 servings

Heat oven to 325°. On a sheet of waxed paper, mix flour, salt, and pepper. Dip steak in flour mixture, turning to coat. In large skillet, melt ¼ cup butter in oil over medium-low heat. Add steak; brown on both sides over medium-high heat. Transfer meat and drippings to 3-quart casserole; set aside.

In large skillet, melt remaining ¼ cup butter over medium-low heat. Add onions, stirring to coat with butter. Cover. Cook until tender but not brown, about 10 minutes. Pour onions over steak in casserole. Add remaining ingredients. Cover. Bake until meat is tender, 2 to 2½ hours. Discard bay leaf before serving.

## Venison Steak Diane  VERY FAST

*Use steaks from the loin or sirloin tip for this recipe. For an elegant touch at a special dinner, prepare this dish tableside on a portable burner.*

　3　tablespoons butter or margarine
¼　cup chopped onion
¾　cup venison stock (page 144) or beef broth
　2　tablespoons red wine
¼　teaspoon sugar
　1　tablespoon freshly ground black pepper
　4　deer, antelope, elk, or moose steaks, ¾ to
　　　　1 inch thick, 6 to 8 ounces each
　3　tablespoons butter or margarine
¼　cup brandy
　　　Fresh parsley for garnish, optional

4 servings

*How to Prepare Venison Steak Diane*

MELT 3 tablespoons butter in medium saucepan over medium heat. Add onion. Cook and stir until golden. Stir in stock, wine, and sugar. Cook until reduced by half.

PLACE pepper on sheet of waxed paper. Coat venison steaks with pepper on both sides, pressing pepper into steaks. Discard excess pepper.

MELT 3 tablespoons butter in medium skillet over medium heat. Add steaks; cook to desired doneness, turning once. Transfer steaks to heated platter; set aside and keep warm.

REMOVE skillet from heat; cool slightly. Add brandy. Heat gently over low heat. Remove from heat. Carefully ignite, using long wooden match. Let stand until flames die.

ADD onion and butter mixture to brandy in skillet. Heat to boiling over medium heat, stirring constantly. Pour sauce over steaks. Garnish platter with parsley.

## Venison Picatta ↑

1¼ pounds deer, antelope, elk, or moose loin
 2 cups milk, divided
 ½ cup all-purpose flour
 ½ teaspoon salt
 ½ teaspoon pepper
 ¼ cup butter or margarine
 ¾ cup dry white wine
 2 to 3 tablespoons fresh lemon juice
 ¼ cup snipped fresh parsley
 1 to 2 tablespoons capers, drained

3 or 4 servings

Slice loin across the grain into thin slices, ¼ inch thick or less.* In shallow dish, combine meat and 1 cup milk. Cover dish with plastic wrap. Refrigerate for 1 to 3 hours. Drain and discard milk. Add remaining 1 cup milk. Let stand at room temperature for 1 hour. Drain and discard milk. Pat venison slices dry with paper towels.

On a sheet of waxed paper, mix flour, salt, and pepper. Dip venison slices in flour mixture, turning to coat. In large skillet, melt butter over medium-high heat. Add venison slices; brown on both sides. Add wine; cook about 2 minutes. Transfer venison slices to heated platter with slotted spoon. Add lemon juice, parsley, and capers to skillet. Reduce heat to medium. Cook, stirring constantly, about 2 minutes, scraping bottom and sides of skillet. Serve sauce over venison slices.

*TIP: The venison will be easier to slice thinly if partially frozen.

## Chicken-Fried Venison Steaks  VERY FAST

*For a down-home meal, serve Chicken-Fried Venison Steaks with black-eyed peas, collard or turnip greens, baking-powder biscuits, and homemade jam.*

1 to 1½ pounds boneless deer, antelope, elk,
   or moose round steak, about ½ inch thick
⅓ cup milk
 1 egg
⅓ cup all-purpose flour
 ½ teaspoon salt
⅛ teaspoon pepper
 2 tablespoons butter or margarine
 2 tablespoons vegetable oil

GRAVY:
1¼ cups milk
 2 tablespoons all-purpose flour
 ¼ teaspoon salt
   Dash pepper

3 or 4 servings

Trim meat; cut into serving-sized pieces. Pound to ¼-inch thickness with meat mallet. In 9-inch pie plate, blend ⅓ cup milk and the egg. On a sheet of waxed paper, mix ⅓ cup flour, ½ teaspoon salt, and ⅛ teaspoon pepper. Dip steaks in milk mixture, then in flour mixture, turning to coat. Set aside.

In large skillet, melt butter in oil over medium-low heat. Add steaks; brown on both sides over medium-high heat. Fry in two batches if necessary. Remove to heated platter. Set aside and keep warm. In small bowl, blend milk into remaining gravy ingredients. Blend into pan drippings. Cook over medium heat, stirring constantly, until thickened and bubbly. Strain if desired. Serve gravy with steaks.

## Old-Fashioned Venison Stew

1½ cups water
½ cup beer
2 envelopes (⅞ ounce each) onion gravy mix
1 tablespoon packed brown sugar
¼ teaspoon ground thyme
2 to 3 pounds deer, antelope, elk, or moose stew meat
3 tablespoons vegetable oil
1 bay leaf
6 carrots, cut into 1-inch pieces
6 medium parsnips, cut into 1-inch cubes
1 cup frozen peas

6 to 8 servings

In small mixing bowl, blend water, beer, gravy mix, brown sugar, and thyme. Set aside. Remove all fat and silverskin from meat. Cut into 1-inch pieces. In Dutch oven, brown meat in oil over medium-high heat. Add beer mixture and bay leaf to Dutch oven. Reduce heat; cover. Simmer until meat is almost tender, 1 to 1½ hours, stirring occasionally. Add carrots and parsnips; re-cover. Cook 20 minutes longer. Add peas; re-cover. Cook 5 to 10 minutes longer. Discard bay leaf before serving.

## Zesty Venison Stew

1 to 2 pounds deer, antelope, elk, or moose stew meat
1 medium onion, chopped
2 tablespoons vegetable oil
2 tablespoons catsup
2 tablespoons currant jelly
2 tablespoons Worcestershire sauce
1 teaspoon salt
¼ cup all-purpose flour
1½ cups venison stock (page 144) or beef broth
1 cup red wine
2 medium potatoes
1 cup sliced carrot
2 cups fresh cauliflowerets

3 to 6 servings

Remove all fat and silverskin from meat. Cut into 1-inch pieces. Set aside. In Dutch oven, cook and stir onion in oil over medium heat until tender. Add catsup, jelly, Worcestershire sauce, and salt. Stir to melt jelly. Blend in flour. Add meat, stock, and wine; stir well. Cover and simmer until meat is almost tender, 1 to 1½ hours. Peel potatoes and cut into 1-inch chunks. Add potatoes and carrot to stew. Cook 20 minutes longer. Add cauliflowerets. Cook until vegetables are tender, about 20 minutes longer.

## Spicy Elk Kabobs  ▷ LOW-FAT →

*Kabobs are also excellent cooked on a charcoal grill.*

MARINADE:
¼ cup finely chopped onion
¼ cup white wine
2 tablespoons vegetable oil
2 tablespoons soy sauce
1 tablespoon packed brown sugar
2 teaspoons ground coriander
1 teaspoon chili powder
½ teaspoon salt
½ teaspoon lemon pepper seasoning
⅛ teaspoon crushed red pepper flakes

1 pound elk steak, cut into 1-inch cubes
2 cups water
1 medium zucchini (6 to 8 ounces), cut into
   ¾-inch slices
1 sweet red pepper, cut into 16 pieces

4 servings

In medium saucepan, combine all marinade ingredients. Heat to boiling, stirring occasionally. Cool to
room temperature. Add elk cubes. Toss to coat with
marinade. Cover; marinate at room temperature
for 30 minutes.

While elk is marinating, heat water to boiling in
medium saucepan. Add zucchini. Return to boiling.
Boil 2 minutes. Drain and rinse under cold water.

With slotted spoon, lift elk cubes from marinade.
Set marinade aside. Divide elk, zucchini, and pepper into four groups. For each kabob, alternate elk
with zucchini and pepper on 12-inch kabob skewer.
Arrange kabobs on broiler pan. Set oven to broil
and/or 550°. Broil kabobs 2 to 3 inches from heat
until meat is desired doneness, 6 to 12 minutes,
turning kabobs and brushing with marinade once.

*Variation:* Substitute deer, antelope, or moose for
the elk.

## Grilled Bacon-Wrapped Big Game ● VERY FAST

*Deer, antelope, elk, moose, or bear is excellent prepared in
this simple fashion. Serve as a main course, or as an
appetizer to a wild-game dinner.*

1 to 1¼ pounds big-game round or rump pieces,
   ¾ to 1 inch thick
4 to 8 slices bacon

2 to 4 servings

Start charcoal briquets in grill. Cut meat into 2-inch-
wide strips. Wrap one or two slices bacon around
each strip. Secure bacon with toothpicks. When
charcoal briquets are covered with ash, spread them
in grill. Place grate above hot coals. Grill meat strips
to desired doneness, 4 to 7 minutes per side.

## Bear Stew ↑

*Although any big-game meat can be used in this recipe, bear meat is particularly good.*

1½ to 2 pounds bear stew meat
 ¼ cup all-purpose flour
 1 teaspoon dried marjoram leaves
 1 teaspoon salt
 ⅛ teaspoon pepper
 2 tablespoons vegetable oil
 1 can (16 ounces) whole tomatoes, undrained
 1 cup water
 ¼ cup white wine or water
 1 tablespoon vinegar
 1 medium onion, cut in half lengthwise and
    thinly sliced
 ½ cup chopped celery
 2 cloves garlic, minced
 1 bay leaf
 2 medium baking potatoes

4 to 6 servings

Remove all fat and silverskin from meat. Cut into 1-inch pieces. In large plastic food-storage bag, combine flour, marjoram, salt, and pepper; shake to mix. Add meat; shake to coat. In heavy medium saucepan, heat oil over medium-high heat until hot. Add meat and flour mixture. Brown, stirring occasionally. Add remaining ingredients except potatoes; mix well. Heat to boiling. Reduce heat; cover. Simmer 1 hour, stirring occasionally.

Cut potatoes into 1-inch chunks. Add to saucepan. Heat to boiling. Reduce heat; cover. Simmer until meat and potatoes are tender, about 1 hour, stirring occasionally. Discard bay leaf before serving.

## Big Game and Onion Casserole Braised in Beer ◆ LOW-FAT

*Serve this casserole with hot buttered egg noodles, a tossed salad, and colorful vegetables.*

SPICE PACKET:
 7 sprigs fresh parsley
 1 bay leaf
 ½ teaspoon dried thyme leaves
 2 whole black peppercorns
 2 whole juniper berries

 2 pounds lean big-game pieces
 2 tablespoons butter or margarine, divided
 2 tablespoons olive oil or vegetable oil, divided
 3 medium onions, sliced
 2 cloves garlic, minced
 2 cups beer
 ⅔ cup venison stock (page 144) or beef broth
 1 tablespoon plus 2 teaspoons packed
    brown sugar
 ¾ teaspoon salt
 ¼ teaspoon pepper
 2 tablespoons cornstarch
 2 tablespoons red wine vinegar

6 to 8 servings

Heat oven to 300°. Place spice-packet ingredients on a 6-inch-square piece of double-thickness cheesecloth. Gather comers; tie closed with kitchen string. Set aside. Remove all fat and silverskin from meat. Cut into pieces about 2 × 3 inches across and ½ inch thick. In large skillet, melt 1 tablespoon butter in 1 tablespoon oil over medium-low heat. Brown meat on both sides over medium-high heat. With slotted spoon, transfer meat to medium mixing bowl or plate; set aside. In same skillet, melt remaining 1 tablespoon butter in 1 tablespoon oil over medium heat. Add onions and garlic. Cook and stir until onions are tender. Remove from heat.

In 3-quart casserole, place one-half of the meat. Top with one-half of the onions. Repeat with remaining meat and onions. Add cheesecloth-wrapped spice packet to casserole. In small mixing bowl, blend beer, stock, brown sugar, salt, and pepper. Pour over casserole ingredients. Cover. Bake until meat is tender, about 2 hours. Remove and discard spice packet.

In small bowl, blend cornstarch and vinegar. Pour into casserole. Stir to blend. Bake uncovered until thickened, about 30 minutes.

## Elk Tenderloin Sauté ↑

*You may substitute moose tenderloin, or deer or antelope loin, for the elk tenderloin in this recipe.*

      2  cups water
      1  teaspoon salt
   ½  pound fresh pearl onions (about 1⅓ cups)
   ¼  cup all-purpose flour
   ½  teaspoon salt
   ¼  teaspoon pepper
   1½  pounds elk tenderloin, thinly sliced
      2  tablespoons butter or margarine
      2  tablespoons vegetable oil
   1¾  cups venison stock (page 144) or beef broth
      1  can (16 ounces) whole tomatoes, cut up
            and drained
   ½  cup burgundy
   ¼  cup tomato paste
      1  teaspoon Worcestershire sauce
   ¼  teaspoon dried thyme leaves
      1  or 2 cloves garlic, minced
      2  bay leaves
   ½  pound fresh mushrooms, cut into halves
            Hot cooked rice or noodles

                                              4 to 6 servings

In small saucepan, heat water and 1 teaspoon salt to boiling. Add onions. Return to boiling. Reduce heat; cover. Simmer until onions are just tender, about 15 minutes. Drain and rinse under cold water. Set aside.

In large plastic food-storage bag, combine flour, ½ teaspoon salt, and the pepper; shake to mix. Add elk slices; shake to coat. In large skillet, melt butter in oil over medium heat. Add elk slices. Cook over medium-high heat until browned but still rare, stirring occasionally. Remove with slotted spoon; set aside. Add remaining ingredients except mushrooms and rice to cooking liquid in skillet; mix well. Add mushrooms and reserved onions. Heat to boiling. Reduce heat; cover. Simmer 10 minutes. Stir in elk slices. Cook, uncovered, over medium-low heat until slightly thickened, about 5 minutes. Discard bay

## Venison Stroganoff  FAST

   1½  to 2 pounds deer, antelope, elk, or
            moose steaks
      2  tablespoons all-purpose flour
   ¾  teaspoon salt
      2  tablespoons butter or margarine
      2  cups sliced fresh mushrooms
      1  cup chopped onion
      2  cloves garlic, minced
   ¼  cup all-purpose flour
   1¾  cups venison stock (page 144) or beef broth
      3  tablespoons sherry
      2  tablespoons tomato paste
   1½  to 2 cups dairy sour cream
            Hot cooked noodles or rice

                                              6 to 8 servings

Remove all fat and silverskin from steaks. Cut into thin strips. In large plastic food-storage bag, combine 2 tablespoons flour and the salt; shake to mix. Add venison strips; shake to coat. In large skillet, melt butter over low heat. Add venison strips. Cook over medium-high heat until browned, stirring constantly. Remove meat with slotted spoon; set aside. Add mushrooms, onion, and garlic to cooking liquid in skillet. Cook and stir over medium heat until onions are just tender. Stir in ¼ cup flour. Blend in stock, sherry, and tomato paste. Heat until bubbly, stirring constantly. Stir in sour cream and venison strips. Heat until just hot; do not boil. Serve over noodles.

## Oven-Method Venison Jerky LOW-FAT

Follow recipe on page 152 for Traditional Venison Jerky, except prepare in oven rather than cold smoker. Jerky will not have smoke flavor. Heat oven to 150°. Prepare meat strips as directed. Place in single layer on cookie-cooling racks (fine-mesh or closely spaced bars work best). Cook meat until dry but not brittle, 4 to 5 hours, rearranging racks once. Use an oven thermometer to be sure oven does not get too warm. Refrigerate jerky for storage.

## Oven-Barbecued Venison Ribs ▷LOW-FAT ↑

SAUCE:

½ cup catsup
½ cup water
¼ cup cider vinegar
¼ cup finely chopped onion
3 tablespoons packed brown sugar
2 tablespoons Worcestershire sauce
1 tablespoon lemon juice
1 tablespoon paprika
1 teaspoon dry mustard
1 teaspoon salt
1 teaspoon liquid smoke flavoring
½ teaspoon pepper
¼ teaspoon chili powder

2 to 3 pounds deer, antelope, elk, or moose ribs
2 cups water

4 servings

In small bowl, combine all sauce ingredients. Mix well. In Dutch oven, combine ribs, 2 cups water, and ¾ cup sauce, reserving remaining sauce. Heat rib mixture to boiling. Reduce heat; cover. Simmer until ribs are tender, about 1 hour, rearranging ribs once or twice.

Heat oven to 350°. Arrange ribs on roasting pan. Brush with reserved sauce. Bake for 10 minutes. Turn ribs over. Brush with sauce. Bake for 10 minutes longer. Serve with remaining sauce.

## Oriental-Style Grilled Venison Ribs ▷LOW-FAT

*Check an Oriental market or the specialty department of a large supermarket for the rice wine vinegar, plum sauce, hoisin sauce, and fresh gingerroot.*

MARINADE:

1½ cups dry sherry
¼ cup peanut oil or vegetable oil
¼ cup rice wine vinegar
6 tablespoons soy sauce
6 tablespoons plum sauce or 3 tablespoons plum jelly
2 tablespoons hoisin sauce
1 tablespoon minced fresh gingerroot
4 cloves garlic, minced

2 to 3 pounds deer, antelope, elk, or moose ribs

4 servings

In medium saucepan, combine all marinade ingredients. Heat over medium heat, stirring constantly, until hot. Cool to room temperature. Place ribs in 13 × 9-inch baking pan, or in an oven cooking bag. Pour cooled marinade over ribs. Cover pan with plastic wrap or seal bag. Marinate ribs for 1 to 2 hours, turning ribs several times.

Start charcoal briquets in grill. When briquets are covered with ash, spread them evenly in grill. Place grate above hot coals. Arrange ribs on grate. Grill until cooked through, 10 to 15 minutes, turning once. Serve with remaining sauce.

## Venison Vegetable Soup  ▷ LOW-FAT →

*After boning your deer, use the meatier bones to make a hearty vegetable soup. Shoulder bones, shanks, and the backbone make particularly good soup. Serve hot crusty rolls and coleslaw with this soup.*

1½ to 2 pounds deer, antelope, elk, or moose
  bones, fairly meaty
 2 stalks celery, thinly sliced
 2 medium carrots, thinly sliced
 1 medium onion, finely chopped
 2 cloves garlic, minced
 2 tablespoons butter or margarine
 3 quarts water
 1 bay leaf
 1 tablespoon salt
 ¾ teaspoon dried marjoram leaves
1½ to 2 cups cubed cooked deer, antelope, elk,
  or moose
 1 can (16 ounces) stewed tomatoes, undrained
 1 package (10 ounces) frozen corn

       About 4 quarts

Heat oven to 400°. Arrange bones in a single layer in large roasting pan or on baking sheet. Bake uncovered until bones are browned, 10 to 20 minutes. Drain, if needed. Set bones aside.

In Dutch oven, cook and stir celery, carrots, onion, and garlic in butter over medium heat until tender. Add browned bones, water, bay leaf, salt, and marjoram. Heat to boiling. Reduce heat; cover. Simmer until meat on bones is very tender, 1½ to 2 hours. Remove bones; cool slightly. Remove meat from bones; discard bones. Return meat to Dutch oven. Add remaining ingredients. Simmer, uncovered, 1 hour longer. Discard bay leaf before serving.

## Orange Onion Liver 🔴 FAST ↑

¼ cup all-purpose flour
⅛ teaspoon salt
⅛ teaspoon pepper
1 pound deer, antelope, elk, or moose liver, trimmed and sliced ½ inch thick
¼ cup butter or margarine
1 medium yellow onion, thinly sliced
1 medium red onion, thinly sliced
1 tablespoon sugar
1 medium orange, sliced
¼ cup butter or margarine
⅓ cup venison stock (page 144) or beef broth
¼ cup brandy
¼ teaspoon dried thyme leaves

3 or 4 servings

Heat oven to 175°. On a sheet of waxed paper, mix flour, salt, and pepper. Dip liver slices in flour mixture, turning to coat. In large skillet, melt ¼ cup butter over medium heat. Add liver slices; brown on both sides. With slotted spoon, transfer to heated serving platter. Keep warm in oven. Add onions to butter in skillet. Cook and stir over medium heat until tender. Set aside and keep warm.

While onions are cooking, place sugar on a sheet of waxed paper. Coat orange slices on both sides. In medium skillet, melt ¼ cup butter over medium heat. Add orange slices. Fry until golden brown, turning once. Remove orange slices; set aside. Add stock, brandy, and thyme to butter in skillet. Cook over low heat for 5 minutes, stirring constantly. Remove from heat. To serve, arrange onions over liver slices. Pour broth mixture over onions and liver. Top with orange slices.

## Venison Liver Pâté

*For a special midnight snack, serve Venison Liver Pâté on hot buttered toast, with a bottle of champagne. This pâté is also great on crackers.*

¼ cup vegetable oil
1 pound deer, antelope, elk, or moose liver, trimmed and cut into 1-inch cubes
2 medium carrots, finely chopped
1 medium onion, finely chopped
3 tablespoons butter or margarine
3 tablespoons snipped fresh parsley
½ teaspoon salt
⅛ teaspoon pepper
⅛ teaspoon ground nutmeg
6 tablespoons butter or margarine, cut up
2 hard-cooked eggs, sliced or chopped, optional

About 1 quart

In large skillet, heat oil over medium-high heat until hot. Add liver. Cook and stir until liver is cooked through, 5 to 7 minutes. Place liver in food processor. Set aside. In large skillet, cook and stir carrots and onion in 3 tablespoons butter over medium heat until tender. Add to liver in food processor. Add remaining ingredients except eggs. Process until smooth, scraping side as needed. Spoon liver mixture into bowl or crock.* Cover with plastic wrap. Refrigerate at least 8 hours. Garnish with eggs.

*TIP: You may spoon mixture into buttered 1-quart mold if desired. Cover with plastic wrap. Refrigerate at least 8 hours. To unmold, remove plastic wrap. Dip mold just up to the edge in sinkful of warm water. Place serving plate on top of mold. Holding mold and plate firmly together, quickly invert. Shake mold gently to free pâté if necessary.

## Fried Deer Heart Slices ⬤ VERY FAST

*Antelope, elk, or moose heart can also be used in this traditional recipe.*

¼ cup all-purpose flour
¼ teaspoon salt
⅛ teaspoon pepper
1 deer heart, sliced ¼ inch thick
   Vegetable oil or bacon drippings

2 to 4 servings

On a sheet of waxed paper, mix flour, salt, and pepper. Dip heart slices in flour mixture, turning to coat. In medium skillet, heat ⅛ inch oil over medium heat until hot. Add heart slices. Fry until browned and cooked through, about 5 minutes, turning once.

## Venison Heart Roast →

1 deer or antelope heart
½ cup all-purpose flour
½ teaspoon salt
⅛ teaspoon pepper
3 to 4 tablespoons bacon fat
4 or 5 slices bacon

3 or 4 servings

*How to Prepare Venison Heart Roast*

SLIP fillet knife lengthwise into outer wall of heart, penetrating only half the thickness of the wall.

SLICE in spiral fashion, from outside to center, "unrolling" heart into one long strip. Remove membranes.

MIX flour, salt, and pepper on a sheet of waxed paper. Dip heart in flour mixture, turning to coat. Heat oven to 325°.

HEAT bacon fat over medium-high heat in large skillet. Brown heart quickly on both sides. Remove from heat. Cool slightly.

LAY 2 or 3 slices bacon on heart. Roll heart jelly-roll style, starting with the short end. Tie securely in two places with kitchen string.

PLACE heart on rack in roasting pan. Cover with 2 slices bacon. Roast until heart is cooked through and tender, about 50 minutes.

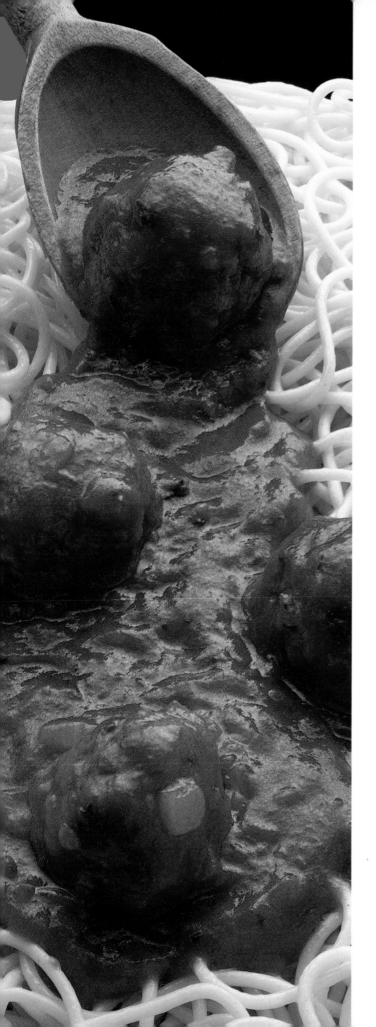

# Italian Meatballs and Sauce

SAUCE:
- 1 can (16 ounces) stewed tomatoes, undrained
- 1 can (6 ounces) tomato paste
- 1 cup burgundy
- 1 medium onion, chopped
- 2 cloves garlic, minced
- 3 tablespoons olive oil
- 1 can (15 ounces) tomato sauce
- 1 tablespoon Italian seasoning
- 1 tablespoon dried parsley flakes
- 1 teaspoon salt
- ½ teaspoon pepper

MEATBALLS:
- 6 slices dry French bread, crust removed
- 2 cups water
- 1 pound big-game burger
- 1 egg, slightly beaten
- 1 clove garlic, minced
- 1 teaspoon Italian seasoning
- ½ teaspoon dried basil leaves
- 2 tablespoons grated Parmesan cheese
- ½ teaspoon salt
- ⅛ teaspoon pepper
- 2 tablespoons bread crumbs, optional
- 3 tablespoons olive oil

Hot cooked spaghetti

4 to 6 servings

In food processor or blender, puree tomatoes. Blend in tomato paste and wine; set aside. In Dutch oven, cook and stir onion and 2 cloves minced garlic in oil over medium-high heat until tender. Add tomato mixture and remaining sauce ingredients. Heat to boiling. Reduce heat to low and cook until sauce thickens and flavors blend, about 2 hours, stirring occasionally.

To prepare meatballs: While sauce is cooking, in medium bowl, combine bread and water. Allow to stand 10 minutes. Drain bread; gently squeeze out excess water. Discard water. Crumble soaked bread into medium mixing bowl. Add meat, egg, 1 clove minced garlic, Italian seasoning, basil, cheese, salt, and pepper. Mix well. If mixture is too soft to hold shape, add bread crumbs, 1 tablespoon at a time. Shape meat mixture into 16 meatballs, about 1½ inches in diameter.

In medium skillet, heat 3 tablespoons oil over medium heat. Add meatballs; brown well on all sides, turning frequently. Remove meatballs with slotted spoon; drain on paper towels. Add meatballs to sauce during last hour of cooking. Serve meatballs and sauce over hot cooked spaghetti.

## Hunter's Favorite Chili ↑

*Set out bowls of shredded Cheddar cheese and sour cream, and plenty of crackers, to top this hearty chili.*

3 pounds big-game burger
3 medium onions, chopped
3 medium green peppers, chopped
½ cup chopped celery
2 tablespoons bacon fat or vegetable oil
1 can (28 ounces) whole tomatoes, undrained
2 tablespoons dried parsley flakes
2 tablespoons chili powder
1 teaspoon salt
1 teaspoon pepper
½ teaspoon garlic powder
2 cans (15½ ounces) kidney beans, undrained
1 can (16 ounces) pinto beans, undrained

8 to 10 servings

In Dutch oven, brown meat over medium heat, stirring occasionally. Remove from heat and set aside. In large skillet, cook and stir onions, green peppers, and celery in bacon fat over medium heat until tender. Add vegetable mixture and all remaining ingredients except beans to meat in Dutch oven. Heat to boiling. Reduce heat; cover. Simmer 1 hour to blend flavors. Stir in beans. Cook, uncovered, 30 minutes longer.

## Hearty Venison Bake FAST

2 cups prepared instant mashed potatoes
⅓ cup butter or margarine, melted
1 pound deer burger or other big-game burger
½ cup chopped onion
2 teaspoons Worcestershire sauce
½ teaspoon salt
⅛ teaspoon pepper
2 eggs
1 cup small-curd cottage cheese
2 medium tomatoes, sliced
1 cup shredded Cheddar cheese

4 to 6 servings

Heat oven to 350°. In medium mixing bowl, combine potatoes and butter; mix well. Set aside ½ cup of the potato mixture. Spread remaining potato mixture in ungreased 9-inch-square baking dish; set aside. In medium skillet, cook meat and onion over medium heat, stirring occasionally, until meat is no longer pink and onion is tender. Drain, if necessary. Stir in Worcestershire sauce, salt, and pepper. Spoon onto potato mixture in baking dish. In small mixing bowl, blend eggs and cottage cheese; pour over meat mixture. Top with tomato slices. Sprinkle with Cheddar cheese. Spread with reserved potato mixture. Bake uncovered until set, about 20 minutes.

## Mexican Enchilada Casserole ↑

2 pounds lean ground deer or other big game
1 medium onion, chopped
2 cloves garlic, minced
1 tablespoon vegetable oil, optional
1 can (8 ounces) tomato sauce
3 tablespoons chili powder
¼ teaspoon salt
1 can (10¾ ounces) cream of chicken soup
¾ cup milk
1 cup shredded Cheddar cheese
1 cup shredded Monterey Jack cheese
1 package (4.8 ounces) taco shells, coarsely
   crushed

8 to 10 servings

Heat oven to 350°. Grease 2-quart casserole; set aside. In large skillet, cook meat, onion, and garlic in oil over medium heat, stirring occasionally, until meat is no longer pink and onion is tender. Drain, if necessary. Stir in tomato sauce, chili powder, and salt. Heat over medium heat until bubbly. Reduce heat to very low; simmer for 10 minutes, stirring occasionally. Remove from heat; set aside.

In small mixing bowl, blend soup and milk; set aside. On a sheet of waxed paper, mix Cheddar and Monterey Jack cheeses; set aside.

In prepared casserole, layer one-third the crushed taco shells, half the meat mixture, half the soup mixture, and half the cheese mixture. Continue layering half the remaining taco shells, the remaining meat mixture, and the remaining soup mixture. Top with the remaining taco shells and the remaining cheese. Bake until hot in the center and cheese melts, about 45 minutes.

## Venison Meatball Pot Pie

1 recipe single pie crust pastry (page 122)*
1 package (5.5 ounces) au gratin potatoes
1 package (10 ounces) frozen peas and carrots,
   thawed and drained
1 pound lean ground deer, antelope, elk,
   or moose
1 cup soft bread crumbs
¼ cup milk
1 egg
2 tablespoons chopped onion
2 tablespoons snipped fresh parsley
¾ teaspoon salt
⅛ teaspoon pepper

4 to 6 servings

Heat oven to 375°. Prepare pie crust as directed. Shape into a ball. Wrap with plastic wrap and refrigerate. Prepare potatoes in 2-quart casserole according to package directions, omitting butter. Add peas and carrots to cooked potatoes; stir to combine. Set aside.

In large mixing bowl, combine remaining ingredients. Mix well. Shape into 16 meatballs, about 1½ inches in diameter. Place meatballs on top of potato mixture. On lightly floured surface, roll out crust slightly larger than top of casserole. Place crust on top of casserole. Turn edge of crust under; flute edge if desired. Cut a small hole in the center of the crust to allow steam to escape. Bake until golden brown, 45 to 55 minutes.

*TIP: Substitute one refrigerated pre-rolled pie crust for homemade crust if desired.

## Quick Venison-Rotini Soup  ●FAST →

1 pound deer, antelope, elk, or moose burger
1 can (16 ounces) whole tomatoes, cut up,
   juice reserved
1 can (8 ounces) tomato sauce
1 envelope (1¾ ounces) chili seasoning mix
4 cups water
1½ cups uncooked rotini noodles
1 package (10 ounces) frozen mixed vegetables
1 tablespoon instant minced onion
1 tablespoon sugar
1 cup dairy sour cream, optional
1 tablespoon dried chives, optional

6 to 8 servings

In Dutch oven, brown meat over medium heat, stirring occasionally. Drain, if necessary. Stir in tomatoes and juice, tomato sauce, and chili seasoning mix. Add water, rotini, vegetables, onion, and sugar; mix well. Heat to boiling. Reduce heat; cover. Simmer until rotini is tender, 10 to 15 minutes. In small mixing bowl, blend sour cream and chives; serve with soup as garnish.

## Swedish Meatballs with Brown Gravy

1 pound big-game burger
⅓ cup milk
⅓ cup instant mashed potato flakes
1 egg, slightly beaten
2 tablespoons finely chopped onion
¾ teaspoon salt
¼ teaspoon ground allspice
⅛ teaspoon ground nutmeg
   Dash pepper
2 tablespoons butter or margarine
1 package (1.8 ounces) dry oxtail soup and
   recipe mix
1½ cups cold water
   Dash ground allspice
   Hot cooked mashed potatoes, optional

4 to 6 servings

In medium mixing bowl, combine meat, milk, potato flakes, egg, onion, salt, ¼ teaspoon allspice, the nutmeg, and pepper. Mix well. Shape into 16 meatballs, about 1½ inches in diameter. In medium skillet, melt butter over medium heat. Add meatballs; brown on all sides, turning frequently. Remove meatballs with slotted spoon; set aside. Stir soup mix into drippings in pan. Blend in water and dash allspice. Cook over medium heat, stirring constantly, until mixture thickens and bubbles. Return meatballs to skillet. Reduce heat; cover. Simmer until meatballs are no longer pink in center, 20 to 30 minutes. Serve with mashed potatoes.

## Venison and Beans ↑

*A great dish to take to a pot-luck supper.*

    6 slices bacon, chopped
1½ pounds deer, antelope, elk, or moose burger
    1 medium onion, chopped
    1 can (16 ounces) pork and beans
    1 can (16 ounces) kidney beans, drained
    1 can (16 ounces) butter beans or Great
        Northern beans, drained
    ⅓ cup packed brown sugar
    1 cup catsup
    2 tablespoons vinegar
    1 tablespoon Worcestershire sauce
    ½ teaspoon salt
    ¼ teaspoon prepared mustard

8 to 10 servings

Heat oven to 350°. In Dutch oven, cook bacon over medium-low heat, stirring occasionally, until crisp. Remove with slotted spoon; set aside. Drain all but 1 tablespoon bacon fat from Dutch oven. Add meat and onion. Cook over medium heat, stirring occasionally, until meat is no longer pink and onion is tender. Add reserved bacon and remaining ingredients to Dutch oven; mix well. Cover and bake until bubbly around edges, about 45 minutes.

## Texas-Style Venison Chili ◆ LOW-FAT

    1 to 1½ pounds boneless deer, moose, or elk
    ¼ cup all-purpose flour
    3 tablespoons bacon fat or vegetable oil
    2 medium onions, chopped
    3 to 5 cloves garlic, minced
    2 or 3 fresh green chilies, minced, or
        ½ to 1 teaspoon dried red pepper flakes
    3 cans (16 ounces) whole tomatoes, undrained
    1 teaspoon dried oregano leaves
    1 teaspoon dried basil leaves
    ½ teaspoon ground cumin
    1 medium green pepper, cut into ¾-inch chunks
        Hot cooked rice

6 to 8 servings

Trim meat if necessary; cut into ½-inch cubes. Place meat cubes and flour in large plastic food-storage bag; shake to coat. In Dutch oven, lightly brown meat in bacon fat over medium-high heat, stirring frequently. Add remaining ingredients except green pepper and rice. Heat to boiling over medium heat. Boil gently for 15 minutes. Reduce heat. Simmer for 1 to 1½ hours, stirring occasionally. Add green pepper. Simmer for 30 minutes longer. Serve over hot cooked rice.

## Venison Meatloaf Supreme ↑

- 2 pounds deer, antelope, elk, or moose burger
- 2 cups soft bread crumbs
- 1/2 cup venison stock (page 144) or beef broth
- 1/2 cup chopped onion
- 2 eggs, slightly beaten
- 1 teaspoon salt
- 1/2 teaspoon Worcestershire sauce
- 1/4 teaspoon sugar
- 1/4 teaspoon celery salt
- 1/4 teaspoon dried crushed sage leaves
- 1/4 teaspoon dried oregano leaves
- 1/4 teaspoon pepper
- 2 small tomatoes, peeled, halved, and seeded

6 to 8 servings

Heat oven to 325°. Grease 9 × 5-inch loaf pan; set aside. In large mixing bowl, combine all ingredients except tomatoes; mix well. Pat half of meat mixture into prepared pan. Arrange tomatoes on meat mixture, leaving 1/2 inch around edges of pan. Spread remaining meat mixture over tomatoes, pressing well around edges to seal. Bake until well browned, about 1 1/2 hours. Let stand 10 minutes. Remove to serving platter.

## Big Game Goulash

- 2 cups uncooked egg noodles
- 1 pound lean ground big game
- 1/2 cup chopped onion
- 1 clove garlic, minced
- 2 tablespoons vegetable oil
- 1 can (16 ounces) whole tomatoes, cut up, juice reserved
- 1 can (16 ounces) kidney beans, drained
- 1 can (8 ounces) tomato sauce
- 1 can (16 ounces) sliced potatoes, drained
- 1 teaspoon salt
- 1 teaspoon dried basil leaves
- 1/4 teaspoon pepper

6 to 8 servings

Heat oven to 350°. Grease a 2-quart casserole; set aside. Cook noodles according to package directions. Rinse and drain. Place in prepared 2-quart casserole; set aside.

In medium skillet, cook meat, onion, and garlic in oil over medium heat, stirring occasionally, until meat is no longer pink and onion is tender. Add meat mixture and remaining ingredients to noodles. Mix well; cover. Bake until hot and bubbly around edges, 35 to 45 minutes.

## Skillet Game Hash  LOW-FAT

*Prepare leftover meat from any big-game roast as a tasty hash. Leftover corned venison (page 85) makes a particularly excellent hash.*

- 1 quart water
- ½ teaspoon salt
- 1½ pounds potatoes
- 1 tablespoon butter
- 2 tablespoons vegetable oil
- ½ cup chopped onion
- 2 cups minced or ground cooked big game
- 1 cup leftover thin game gravy
- ½ teaspoon salt
- ¼ teaspoon dried basil leaves
- ¼ teaspoon pepper
- ⅛ teaspoon dried thyme leaves
  Dash nutmeg
  Dash garlic powder

4 to 6 servings

In medium saucepan, heat water and ½ teaspoon salt to boiling. Add potatoes. Return to boiling. Reduce heat; cover. Simmer until tender, 20 to 25 minutes. Cool. Peel and cut into ½-inch cubes.

In large skillet, melt butter in oil over medium-high heat. Add potatoes and onion. Cook, stirring frequently, until potatoes are lightly browned and onion is tender. Remove from heat. Add remaining ingredients. Mix well. Cover and cook over low heat for 5 minutes to heat through and blend flavors.

## Big Game Sandwich Filling LOW-FAT VERY FAST

- 2 cups diced cooked big game
- 1 can (4½ ounces) deviled ham
- ¼ cup coarsely chopped onion
- ¼ teaspoon salt
- ⅛ teaspoon pepper
- ¼ to ½ cup venison stock (page 144) or beef broth

2¼ cups

In food processor,* combine game, deviled ham, onion, salt, and pepper. Chop to desired consistency. Add stock gradually to chopped meat until moistened to spreadable consistency.

*TIP: You may prepare Big Game Sandwich Filling with meat grinder instead of food processor. In large mixing bowl, combine game, deviled ham, onion, salt, and pepper. Mix well. Grind to desired consistency. Add stock gradually to ground meat until moistened to spreadable consistency.

## Big Game Pie ↑

*If you're short on time, use two refrigerated pre-rolled pie crusts instead of the homemade crust. Remove one of the crusts from its foil pan, and use it for the top crust.*

DOUBLE PIE CRUST PASTRY:
- 2 cups all-purpose flour
- 1 teaspoon salt
- ⅔ cup shortening
- 3 tablespoons butter or margarine, room temperature
- 5 to 7 tablespoons cold water

FILLING:
- 2 cups cut-up cooked big game
- 1½ cups thinly sliced potato
- ½ cup thinly sliced carrot
- ½ cup cubed rutabaga, ½-inch cubes
- 1 small onion, thinly sliced and separated into rings
- 1 package (.75 ounce) herb-flavored brown gravy mix, or 1 cup leftover game gravy
- ¼ teaspoon salt
- ⅛ teaspoon pepper
- 1 tablespoon butter or margarine, cut up

GLAZE: (optional)
- 1 egg
- 1 tablespoon water

4 to 6 servings

## How to Prepare Big Game Pie

COMBINE flour and salt in medium mixing bowl. Cut shortening and 3 tablespoons butter into flour until particles resemble coarse crumbs.

SPRINKLE flour mixture with cold water while tossing with fork, until particles just cling together. Divide into two balls. Heat oven to 375°.

ROLL one ball on lightly floured board into thin circle at least 2 inches larger than inverted 9-inch pie plate. Fit pastry into pie plate. Trim overhang.

LAYER meat, potato, carrot, rutabaga, and onion in pastry shell. Prepare gravy mix according to package directions, adding ¼ teaspoon salt and the pepper. Pour into pie.

DOT pie filling with butter. Roll out remaining pastry. Place on filling. Seal and flute edges. If desired, roll out pastry scraps; cut into decorations and place on pastry top.

CUT several slits in pastry top. In small bowl, blend glaze ingredients. Brush over pastry top. Bake until crust is golden brown, about 1 hour. Let stand 10 minutes before serving.

# Big-Game Sausage

Fresh big-game sausage is surprisingly easy to make at home. All recipes in this section are for uncased sausages, and require no special equipment other than a food processor or meat grinder.

You can use any big-game cut to make sausage. The best choices are cuts that might be tough if cooked whole. Scraps left after cutting up a big-game animal work well.

Fatty pork is usually added to the trimmed game meat to make sausage. If you prefer sausage with game meat only, you still need to add fat. Ask your butcher for hard pork or beef fat from the outside of the loin. A ratio of one part fat to three or four parts game meat produces a juicy, flavorful sausage. To produce the best texture, keep the fat and meat very cold during chopping or grinding.

Experiment with small batches to find a sausage recipe you like. Then double or triple the recipe to make a big batch. It's best to underseason sausage somewhat, then fry up a small patty and taste it. Add additional seasonings or salt if necessary.

Any of the sausage recipes in this book can also be used to make cased sausages. You'll need casings, available from some butcher shops, and a sausage stuffer. Follow the instructions that come with the stuffer. Cased sausages can be cold-smoked (page 149) for 2 or 3 hours to add additional flavor.

Summer sausage and other cured or dried sausages are more difficult to make than the fresh sausages in this book. If you know how to make cured sausages, you can substitute game meat for beef.

## Sweet Italian Sausage

1 pound trimmed deer or other big-game meat
1 pound boneless fatty pork shoulder or
    pork butt
1 teaspoon salt
1 teaspoon sugar
½ teaspoon garlic powder
½ teaspoon fennel seed

½ teaspoon lemon pepper seasoning
½ teaspoon paprika
¼ teaspoon celery salt
¼ teaspoon dried crushed sage leaves
⅛ teaspoon cayenne
1 tablespoon soy sauce
½ teaspoon Worcestershire sauce

2 pounds

*How to Prepare Sweet Italian Sausage*

CUT the deer and pork into ¾-inch cubes. Place in medium mixing bowl; set aside.

MIX remaining ingredients except soy sauce and Worcestershire sauce; sprinkle over meat. Toss to coat.

SPRINKLE soy and Worcestershire sauces over meat; mix. Cover. Refrigerate 8 hours or overnight.

CHOP meat mixture to medium consistency in food processor, or grind with medium plate of meat grinder.

FRY a small patty over medium heat to check seasoning. Adjust salt and other seasonings if necessary.

USE sausage for pizza topping, meatballs for spaghetti, or breakfast patties. Sausage also freezes well.

## Mexican Chorizo Sausage ↑

*Boldly flavored, this sausage can be used for tacos, chili, or tiny appetizer meatballs.*

  2 pounds trimmed deer or other big-game meat
  2 pounds boneless fatty pork shoulder or
       pork butt
  2 tablespoons paprika
  1 tablespoon salt
  1 tablespoon black pepper
  2 teaspoons crushed red pepper flakes
  1 teaspoon sugar
  1 teaspoon garlic powder
  ½ teaspoon dried oregano leaves
  ¼ teaspoon cumin seed
  ¼ cup white vinegar

About 4 pounds

Cut deer and pork into ¾-inch cubes. Place in large mixing bowl. In small bowl, mix remaining ingredients except vinegar. Sprinkle over meat; mix well. Chop or grind to medium consistency. Return meat mixture to large mixing bowl. Add vinegar; mix well. Cover bowl tightly with plastic wrap. Refrigerate for at least one hour to blend flavors. Cook over medium heat, stirring occasionally, until brown; use for tacos or chili. Or, shape into tiny meatballs or patties, and fry over medium heat until browned and cooked through, turning to brown all sides. Sausage can also be frozen uncooked.

## Garlic Sausage

*Serve patties of Garlic Sausage as a main course with a hearty soup, tossed salad, and French bread. This sausage is also excellent on pizzas or in chili.*

  1½ pounds boneless fatty pork shoulder or
       pork butt
  1 pound trimmed deer or other big-game meat
  3 to 4 teaspoons fresh minced garlic
  1 tablespoon salt
  1 teaspoon pepper
  ½ cup water

About 3 pounds

Cut pork and deer into ¾-inch cubes. Place in large mixing bowl. Sprinkle garlic, salt, and pepper over meat; mix well. Chop or grind to medium consistency. Return meat mixture to large mixing bowl. Add water; mix well. Cover bowl tightly with plastic wrap. Refrigerate for two days to blend flavors and allow garlic to mellow. Shape into thin patties and fry over medium heat until browned and cooked through, turning once. Sausage can also be frozen uncooked after two-day blending period.

## Venison Breakfast Sausage  FAST

1 pound trimmed deer or other big-game meat
6 ounces lean bacon ends or slab bacon
¾ teaspoon salt
1 teaspoon dried crushed sage leaves
½ teaspoon ground ginger
¼ teaspoon pepper

1½ pounds

Cut the deer and bacon into ¾-inch cubes. Place in medium mixing bowl. In small bowl, mix salt, sage, ginger, and pepper. Sprinkle over meat; mix well. Chop or grind to desired consistency. Shape into thin patties and fry over medium heat until browned and cooked through, turning once. Sausage can also be frozen uncooked.

## Potato Sausage   LOW-FAT

*Fry this sausage in patties for breakfast, brunch, or dinner, or use it to make an interesting meatloaf.*

1 quart water
2 pounds peeled red potatoes
1 pound trimmed deer, antelope, elk, or moose
1 pound boneless fatty pork shoulder or
   pork butt
1 medium onion, coarsely chopped
1 egg, beaten
1 tablespoon salt
½ teaspoon ground allspice
¼ teaspoon dried ground sage leaves
¼ teaspoon dried basil leaves
¼ teaspoon sugar

4 pounds

In 2-quart saucepan, heat water to boiling. Add potatoes. Return to boiling. Reduce heat; cover. Simmer until potatoes are fork-tender, 25 to 35 minutes. Drain. Cool potatoes; cut into ¾-inch cubes.

Cut deer and pork into ¾-inch cubes. In large mixing bowl, combine deer, pork, potato cubes, onion, and egg. In small bowl, mix remaining ingredients. Sprinkle over meat and potato mixture; mix well. Cover bowl tightly with plastic wrap. Refrigerate at least 1 hour to blend flavors.

Chop or grind meat and potato mixture to medium consistency. Shape into thin patties. Fry in non-stick skillet over medium-low heat in a small amount of vegetable oil until browned and cooked through, turning once.

# Big-Game Mincemeat

Once you make your own big-game mincemeat. you may never use canned mincemeat again. Homemade mincemeat is delicious, and fills the house with the smell of the holidays. Use homemade mincemeat exactly as you would the commercial variety. Try it as a filling for cookies or tarts, as a warm topping for ice cream, and of course as the main ingredient in the traditional holiday pie.

## Venison Mincemeat ▷ LOW-FAT

       2  pounds lean ground deer, antelope, elk, or moose (uncooked)
     1/4  pound beef suet, ground medium-fine
       5  cups seedless dark or golden raisins
       4  cups chopped tart apple
       3  cups apple cider
       2  cups currants
       2  cups packed brown sugar
    1 1/2  cups granulated sugar
       1  package (8 ounces) chopped citron
     3/4  cup cider vinegar
     1/2  to 1 cup coarsely chopped slivered almonds
          Grated peel from 3 or 4 oranges
       2  teaspoons salt
       2  teaspoons ground cinnamon
    1 1/2  teaspoons ground nutmeg
       1  teaspoon ground cloves
       1  teaspoon ground mace
       1  teaspoon ground allspice
     1/4  cup brandy or rum, optional

About 4 quarts

In large Dutch oven or stock pot, combine all ingredients except brandy. Mix well. Heat to boiling, stirring frequently. Reduce heat; cover. Simmer 2 hours, stirring occasionally. Cool. Stir brandy into mincemeat. Place mincemeat into pint- or quart-sized containers for storage. Mincemeat can be stored in the refrigerator for 3 or 4 days, or frozen for up to a year. Mincemeat may also be canned in a pressure cooker (page 153); process pint jars for 60 minutes at 10 pounds pressure.

*Variation:* Substitute 2 ounces ground suet (about 1/2 cup) and 1/4 cup butter for 1/4 pound suet.

## Big-Game Mincemeat Pie ↑

    4  to 5 cups venison mincemeat
    1  recipe double pie crust pastry (page 78)
    1  egg
    1  tablespoon water

9-inch pie

Prepare mincemeat and pie crust as directed. Heat oven to 425°. On lightly floured board, roll one-half of pastry into thin circle at least 2 inches larger than inverted 9-inch pie plate. Fit crust into pie plate, pressing gently against bottom and side. Trim overhang 1/2 inch from rim. Fill with mincemeat. Roll out remaining pastry. Place on filling. Seal and flute edges. If desired, roll out pastry scraps; cut into decorations and place on pastry top. Cut several slits in pastry top. Blend egg and water. Brush over top. Bake at 425° for 10 minutes. Reduce heat to 350° and continue baking until crust is golden brown, 35 to 45 minutes.

# Corning Big Game

Corning is a method of meat preservation developed in the days before refrigeration. After butchering a steer, a farmer would cure the brisket or some other tough cut in a salt-sugar brine for several weeks. The salt acted as a preservative, and the sugar developed flavor and tenderness. Meat cured this way was called "corned" because the salt pellets were about the size of corn kernels.

On a moose or elk the *brisket,* or thin meat that covers the bottom of the rib cage, is thick enough for corning. But on smaller animals like antelope and deer, it may be too thin. Flank meat, which lies between the last rib and the hindquarter, is also a good choice, as is the shoulder roast.

The corning recipe below requires two types of salt. *Canning and pickling salt* is pure salt, without any iodine or free-flowing agents which might adversely affect the texture of the meat. *Tenderizing salt* is a mixture of salt, sugar, and preservatives. It adds flavor and tenderness, and the preservatives give the meat its characteristic pink color.

## Corned Venison  ⬧ LOW-FAT

2 to 3-pound brisket, flank, or shoulder roast up to 1 inch thick
2 quarts spring water or distilled water
½ cup canning and pickling salt
½ cup tenderizing salt (e.g. Morton's Tenderquick®)
3 tablespoons sugar
2 tablespoons mixed pickling spice
2 bay leaves
8 whole black peppercorns
1 or 2 cloves garlic, minced

4 to 6 servings

Roll brisket or flank loosely and tie (page 25). Place in large glass or pottery mixing bowl, or in large oven cooking bag. In glass or enamel saucepan, combine remaining ingredients. Heat just to boiling. Remove from heat; cool. Pour cooled brine over meat. Cover bowl with plastic wrap; or, if using oven cooking bag, squeeze to remove air, then twist neck of bag and seal. Refrigerate 4 to 5 days, turning meat occasionally. Drain. Rinse meat with cold water.

To prepare corned meat, place in Dutch oven. Cover with cold water. Heat to boiling; drain. Cover with cold water. Heat to boiling. Reduce heat; cover. Simmer until tender, 3½ to 4½ hours.

## Corned Venison with Vegetables  ⬧ LOW-FAT ↑

2 to 3-pound uncooked corned venison roast
5 carrots, cut into 2-inch pieces
4 medium red potatoes, quartered
2 medium onions, quartered
1 small head cabbage (about 1¼ pounds), cored and quartered

6 to 8 servings

Drain and rinse corned meat in cold water as directed. Place in Dutch oven. Cover with cold water. Heat to boiling; drain. Cover with cold water. Heat to boiling. Reduce heat; cover. Simmer until almost tender, 2¾ to 3¾ hours. Add carrots; re-cover. Simmer for 20 minutes longer. Add potatoes, onions, and cabbage; re-cover. Simmer until meat and vegetables are tender, about 30 minutes longer.

# Cooking Small Game

The taste and texture of small-game animals vary greatly. Squirrel meat, for example, is mild and light-colored with a velvety texture, while raccoon is rich, dark, and coarse-fibered.

The age of an animal also affects taste and texture, which in turn affect the cooking method. Young squirrels are delicious when fried; old ones would be tough and are better stewed or simmered. Rabbits, because of their short life span, are usually tender. Hares, whether young or old, are tougher and gamier, and usually are marinated or stewed to tenderize the meat and diminish the strong flavor. A young raccoon is tasty and tender when roasted, but an old one dressing out at 10 pounds or more is likely to be strong and tough, regardless of cooking method.

To ensure tenderness, most of the recipes in this section rely on braising or other moist, slow-cooking methods. Pressure-cooking also tenderizes quickly and easily, and is usually the best way to cook old small-game animals.

To prepare a small-game dinner, you need about ¾ pound of dressed game per person. Gray squirrels dress out at about ¾ pound, fox squirrels 1 pound, cottontail rabbits 1½ to 2 pounds, snowshoe hares 2½ to 3 pounds, and young raccoons 3 to 6 pounds.

## How to Cook Small Game in a Pressure Cooker

### Pressure-Cooking Times for Small Game

| TYPE OF GAME | COOKING TIME (At 15 Pounds Pressure) |
| --- | --- |
| Squirrel, young | 15 minutes |
| Squirrel, old | 20 minutes |
| Cottontail Rabbit | 20 minutes |
| Snowshoe Hare | 25 minutes |
| Raccoon, young | 20-25 minutes |
| Raccoon, old | 30 minutes |

Always follow manufacturer's directions when using your pressure cooker. Consult manual for specific recommendations.

You may heat oil in your pressure cooker and brown the game before pressure-cooking if desired. Add water carefully to browned game, and seal cooker immediately to prevent water loss.

PLACE cut-up game in the pressure cooker, on a trivet if desired. Do not exceed two-thirds of the cooker's capacity. Add 1 to 1½ inches of water, or the amount specified in the cooker manual. Seal the cooker, then set the control for 15 pounds of pressure.

HEAT to full pressure as directed by the manual. Normally, the control starts to jiggle when full pressure is reached. Begin timing, then lower the heat so the control jiggles only one to four times per minute.

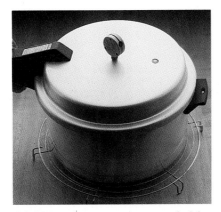

COOK as long as recommended by the chart (above left), then remove the cooker from the heat. Do not remove the control or open the cooker until it cools completely. Escaping steam could cause serious burns.

COOL according to the pressure-cooker manual. Generally, the cooker is allowed to cool naturally for about 5 minutes, then is placed under cold running water until it's cool enough to touch. Remove meat with tongs.

## Brunswick Stew ↓

¼ cup all-purpose flour
1 teaspoon salt
¼ to ½ teaspoon pepper
3 squirrels, cut up
2 slices bacon, cut up
2 tablespoons butter or margarine
5 cups water
1 can (28 ounces) whole tomatoes, drained
1 medium onion, chopped
1 tablespoon packed brown sugar
2 medium potatoes
1 package (10 ounces) frozen lima beans
1 cup fresh or frozen whole-kernel corn
3 tablespoons all-purpose flour, optional
3 tablespoons cold water, optional

6 to 8 servings

In large plastic food-storage bag, combine ¼ cup flour, the salt, and pepper; shake to mix. Add squirrel pieces; shake to coat. Set aside. In Dutch oven, combine bacon and butter. Heat over medium heat until butter melts. Add squirrel pieces; brown on all sides. Fry in two batches if necessary. Add 5 cups water, the tomatoes, onion, and brown sugar. Heat to boiling. Reduce heat; cover. Simmer until squirrel pieces are tender, 1½ to 2 hours, stirring occasionally.

Remove squirrel pieces; set aside to cool slightly. Cut potatoes into ½-inch cubes. Remove squirrel meat from bones; discard bones. Add squirrel meat, potatoes, beans, and corn to Dutch oven. Heat to boiling. Reduce heat; cover. Simmer until potatoes are tender, 25 to 35 minutes. If stew is thinner than desired, blend 3 tablespoons flour and 3 tablespoons cold water in small bowl. Add to stew, stirring constantly. Heat to boiling. Cook over medium heat, stirring constantly, until thickened and bubbly.

## Homesteaders' Rabbit or Squirrel with Cream Gravy

*This is based on an old recipe from a Swiss settlement in Wisconsin. Serve with mashed potatoes, pickled beets, green salad, bread, gooseberry jam, and thick-sliced Swiss cheese, with cherry pie for dessert.*

3 tablespoons all-purpose flour
½ teaspoon salt
⅛ teaspoon pepper
⅛ teaspoon ground nutmeg
1 wild rabbit or 2 squirrels, cut up
2 tablespoons butter or margarine
2 tablespoons vegetable oil
¾ cup rabbit stock (page 145) or chicken broth
½ cup chopped onion
1 small bay leaf
½ cup half-and-half

2 or 3 servings

In large plastic food-storage bag, combine flour, salt, pepper, and nutmeg; shake to mix. Add rabbit pieces; shake to coat. Reserve excess flour mixture. In large skillet, melt butter in oil over medium-low heat. Add coated rabbit pieces and excess flour mixture. Brown rabbit pieces on all sides over medium-high heat. Add stock, onion, and bay leaf. Heat to boiling. Reduce heat; cover. Simmer until meat is tender, 45 minutes to 1 hour for rabbit, about 1½ hours for squirrel. Stir in cream. Cook over medium-low heat until cream is heated through; do not boil. Discard bay leaf before serving.

*Variation:* Follow recipe above, substituting ½ cup white wine and ¼ cup water for the rabbit stock. Substitute ⅓ cup dairy sour cream for the half-and-half. Proceed as directed above.

## Sherried Squirrel or Rabbit ↑

4 squirrels or 2 wild rabbits, cut up
2 quarts water
1 tablespoon salt
2 teaspoons vinegar
⅓ cup all-purpose flour
1 teaspoon salt
⅛ teaspoon pepper
2 tablespoons butter or margarine
2 tablespoons vegetable oil
8 ounces fresh whole mushrooms

SHERRY SAUCE:
1 cup rabbit stock (page 145) or chicken broth
¼ cup sherry
1 tablespoon Worcestershire sauce
¼ teaspoon seasoned salt
2 or 3 drops hot red pepper sauce

4 to 6 servings

In large glass or ceramic bowl, combine squirrel pieces, water, 1 tablespoon salt, and the vinegar. Cover bowl with plastic wrap. Let stand at room temperature 1 hour. Drain, discarding liquid. Pat squirrel pieces dry; set aside.

Heat oven to 350°. In large plastic food-storage bag, combine flour, 1 teaspoon salt, and the pepper; shake to mix. Add squirrel pieces; shake to coat. In large skillet, melt butter in oil over medium-low heat. Add squirrel pieces; brown on all sides over medium-high heat. Transfer squirrel pieces and drippings to 3-quart casserole. Add mushrooms. In 2-cup measure, combine all sherry sauce ingredients. Pour over squirrel pieces and mushrooms. Cover casserole. Bake until tender, about 1½ hours.

## Southern Fried Squirrel or Rabbit with Gravy

⅓ cup all-purpose flour
½ teaspoon salt
⅛ teaspoon black pepper
⅛ teaspoon cayenne pepper, optional
2 squirrels or 1 wild rabbit, cut up
Vegetable oil
3 tablespoons all-purpose flour
1½ cups milk or chicken broth
Salt and pepper
Brown bouquet sauce, optional

2 or 3 servings

In large plastic food-storage bag, combine ⅓ cup flour, the salt, black pepper, and cayenne pepper; shake to mix. Add squirrel pieces; shake to coat. In large skillet, heat ⅛ inch oil for squirrel, or ¼ inch oil for rabbit, over medium-high heat until hot. Add coated meat; brown on all sides. Reduce heat; cover tightly. Cook over very low heat until tender, 35 to 45 minutes for squirrel, 20 to 25 minutes for rabbit, turning pieces once. Remove cover; cook 5 minutes longer to crisp. Transfer meat to plate lined with paper towels. Set aside and keep warm.

Discard all but 3 tablespoons oil. Over medium heat, stir flour into reserved oil. Blend in milk. Cook over medium heat, stirring constantly, until thickened and bubbly. Add salt and pepper to taste. Add bouquet sauce if darker color is desired. Serve gravy with meat.

## ← Oven-Barbecued Rabbit

BARBECUE SAUCE:
2 medium onions, finely chopped
2 green peppers, finely chopped
1 clove garlic, minced
1 cup water
1 cup cider vinegar
½ cup catsup
½ cup packed brown sugar
¼ cup butter or margarine, cut up
2 tablespoons Worcestershire sauce
1 teaspoon salt
½ teaspoon cayenne pepper

2 wild rabbits, cut up

4 to 6 servings

Heat oven to 300°. In medium saucepan, combine all barbecue sauce ingredients. Cook over medium-high heat until bubbly, stirring occasionally. Reduce heat. Simmer 10 minutes. Arrange rabbit pieces in single layer in 13 × 9-inch baking pan. Pour sauce evenly over rabbit pieces. Bake until tender, 2½ to 3 hours, turning rabbit pieces occasionally.

## Rabbit in Apple Cider

1 tablespoon butter or margarine
1 tablespoon vegetable oil
1 wild rabbit, cut up
1 medium onion, cut into eighths
2 medium carrots, diced
1½ cups apple cider
½ teaspoon salt
¼ teaspoon dried thyme leaves
1 bay leaf
4 whole black peppercorns
2 medium cooking apples

2 or 3 servings

In Dutch oven, melt butter in oil over medium-low heat. Add rabbit pieces; brown well on all sides over medium-high heat. Remove rabbit pieces with slotted spoon; set aside. Add onion and carrots to oil. Cook and stir over medium heat until tender. Stir in cider, salt, thyme, bay leaf, and peppercorns. Heat to boiling. Add browned rabbit pieces. Reduce heat; cover. Simmer until rabbit pieces are tender, 50 minutes to 1 hour. Core and quarter apples. Add to rabbit pieces. Re-cover. Simmer until apples are just tender, 10 to 15 minutes. Discard bay leaf before serving. If desired, transfer rabbit pieces, vegetables, and apples to serving platter with slotted spoon.

## Rabbit Stew →

- ¼ cup olive oil
- 1 wild rabbit, cut up
- 1 medium onion, chopped
- 2 shallots, finely chopped
- 1 can (16 ounces) stewed tomatoes, undrained
- ½ cup red wine
- 1½ cups sliced fresh mushrooms
- 2 medium carrots, sliced
- 2 tablespoons brandy
- 2 tablespoons snipped fresh parsley
- 1 teaspoon dried oregano leaves
- 1 teaspoon dried rosemary leaves
- ½ teaspoon salt
- ¼ teaspoon pepper
- 1 cup pitted black olives

2 or 3 servings

In Dutch oven, heat oil over medium-high heat. Add rabbit pieces; brown on all sides. Remove rabbit pieces with slotted spoon; set aside. Add onion and shallots to oil. Cook and stir over medium heat until tender. Add browned rabbit pieces and remaining ingredients except olives. Mix well; cover. Cook over medium heat until rabbit is tender, 50 minutes to 1 hour, turning rabbit pieces occasionally. Add olives; re-cover. Cook about 10 minutes longer.

## Oven-Braised Rabbit with Gravy

*Rice pilaf, cranberry relish, and corn muffins with honey complete this meal.*

- ½ cup all-purpose flour
- 1 teaspoon salt
- ⅛ teaspoon pepper
- ⅛ teaspoon garlic powder
- 2 wild rabbits, cut up
- 1 tablespoon butter or margarine
- 3 tablespoons vegetable oil
- 8 ounces fresh mushrooms, sliced
- 1 cup sliced carrot
- 1 cup sliced celery
- 1 medium onion, sliced
- 2 tablespoons snipped fresh parsley or
    2 teaspoons dried parsley flakes
- ¼ teaspoon dried thyme leaves
- 1 large bay leaf
- 1 cup rabbit stock (page 145) or chicken broth
- 1 cup white wine
- 3 tablespoons milk

4 to 6 servings

Heat oven to 350°. In large plastic food-storage bag, combine flour, salt, pepper, and garlic powder; shake to mix. Add rabbit pieces; shake to coat. Reserve excess flour mixture. In Dutch oven, melt butter in oil over medium-high heat. Add coated rabbit pieces; brown well on all sides. Remove from heat. Add remaining ingredients except milk and reserved flour mixture. Cover; bake until rabbit pieces are tender, about 1½ hours.

With slotted spoon, transfer rabbit pieces and vegetables to heated serving platter. Set aside and keep warm. Discard bay leaf. In small bowl, blend 2 to 3 tablespoons reserved flour mixture into milk to form a thin paste. Blend a small amount of milk mixture into cooking liquid. Cook over medium heat, stirring constantly, until thickened and bubbly. Add additional milk mixture if thicker gravy is desired. Cook and stir until desired consistency. Serve gravy with rabbit and vegetables.

*Variation:* Follow recipe above, substituting rabbit stock or chicken broth for the white wine.

## Rabbit Braised with Bacon and Mushrooms ↑

*An interesting blend of flavors makes this dish special. Serve with buttered noodles and sauerkraut, with baked apples for dessert.*

    8  slices bacon, cut up
  ⅓  cup all-purpose flour
  ½  teaspoon salt
  ⅛  teaspoon pepper
    1  wild rabbit, cut up
    2  tablespoons butter or margarine
    1  cup red wine
    1  medium onion, chopped
  ¼  cup brandy
  ¼  cup applesauce
    1  tablespoon red wine vinegar
    1  tablespoon Dijon mustard
    2  cloves garlic, minced
1½  cups sliced fresh mushrooms
       Salt and freshly ground black pepper

2 or 3 servings

In large skillet, cook bacon over medium heat until crisp, stirring occasionally. Remove skillet from heat. Remove bacon with slotted spoon; set aside. Reserve 2 tablespoons bacon fat in skillet.

In large plastic food-storage bag, combine flour, salt, and pepper; shake to mix. Add rabbit pieces; shake to coat. Melt butter in reserved bacon fat in skillet over medium-low heat. Add coated rabbit pieces; brown well on all sides over medium-high heat. Remove rabbit pieces with slotted spoon. Add wine, onion, brandy, applesauce, vinegar, mustard, and garlic. Mix well. Return rabbit pieces to skillet. Heat to boiling. Reduce heat; cover. Simmer 45 minutes, turning rabbit pieces occasionally. Add mushrooms and cooked bacon. Re-cover. Simmer until rabbit pieces are tender, 10 to 20 minutes longer. Add salt and pepper to taste.

## Rabbit with Dumplings

  ¼  cup all-purpose flour
  ¼  teaspoon salt
  ¼  teaspoon pepper
    1  wild rabbit, cut up
    3  tablespoons vegetable oil
2¼  cups rabbit stock (page 145) or chicken broth
    2  teaspoons paprika
    1  or 2 cloves garlic, minced

DUMPLINGS:
    1  cup all-purpose flour
    2  tablespoons snipped fresh parsley or
         2 teaspoons dried parsley flakes
    1  teaspoon instant minced onion
  ¾  teaspoon salt
    1  egg
  ½  cup milk

    4  cups water
    1  cup dairy sour cream

2 or 3 servings

In large plastic food-storage bag, combine ¼ cup flour, ¼ teaspoon salt, and the pepper; shake to mix. Add rabbit pieces; shake to coat. In Dutch oven, heat oil over medium-high heat. Add coated rabbit pieces; brown on all sides. Add stock, paprika, and garlic. Heat to boiling. Reduce heat; cover. Simmer until rabbit pieces are tender, 50 minutes to 1 hour.

In medium mixing bowl, combine all dumpling ingredients except milk; mix well. Blend in milk, a little at a time, until moistened. Set aside. In large skillet, heat 4 cups water to boiling. Drop dough, about 2 tablespoons at a time, into boiling water. Boil 10 minutes, turning once. With slotted spoon, transfer dumplings to colander. Rinse with hot water; drain. Add to rabbit pieces. Re-cover. Cook over medium heat about 5 minutes. Reduce heat to low. Blend in sour cream. Cook, uncovered, until heated through, about 5 minutes; do not boil.

## Spanish Rabbit →

3 tablespoons olive oil
1 wild rabbit, cut up
2 medium onions, chopped
1 green pepper, cut into ½-inch pieces
2 cloves garlic, minced
2 cups rabbit stock (page 145) or chicken broth
1 cup uncooked long grain rice
½ cup snipped fresh parsley
¼ teaspoon salt
¼ teaspoon crushed saffron threads
¼ teaspoon pepper
2 medium tomatoes, seeded, chopped,
   and drained
1 cup large pitted black olives
1 jar (2 ounces) diced pimiento, drained

2 or 3 servings

In Dutch oven, heat oil over medium heat. Add rabbit pieces. Fry 10 minutes, turning pieces over once. Remove with slotted spoon; set aside. Add onions, green pepper, and garlic to oil. Cook and stir until tender. Add rabbit pieces, stock, rice, parsley, salt, saffron, and pepper. Heat to boiling. Reduce heat; cover. Simmer until rice is tender and liquid is absorbed, 45 to 55 minutes. Stir in tomatoes, olives, and pimiento. Re-cover. Cook until heated through, about 5 minutes.

## Tomato-Rabbit Casserole

1 tablespoon butter or margarine
1 tablespoon vegetable oil
1 wild rabbit, cut up
3 medium potatoes, quartered
4 to 6 small onions
1 can (16 ounces) whole tomatoes, undrained
1 cup vegetable juice cocktail
1 bay leaf
½ teaspoon salt
½ teaspoon dried basil leaves
¼ teaspoon dried tarragon leaves
¼ teaspoon pepper

2 or 3 servings

Heat oven to 350°. In medium skillet, melt butter in oil over medium-low heat. Add rabbit pieces; brown on all sides over medium-high heat. Transfer rabbit pieces to 3-quart casserole. Add remaining ingredients; mix well. Cover; bake until rabbit pieces are tender, about 1½ hours. Discard bay leaf before serving.

## Cranberry Braised Raccoon

2½ to 3 pounds raccoon pieces, fat and
   glands removed
 1 cup finely chopped cranberries
 1 cup apple cider
¼ cup honey
 1 teaspoon grated orange peel
¾ teaspoon salt
⅛ teaspoon ground cloves
⅛ teaspoon ground nutmeg

3 or 4 servings

Place raccoon pieces in large saucepan. In small
mixing bowl, combine remaining ingredients; mix
well. Pour over raccoon pieces. Heat to boiling.
Reduce heat; cover. Simmer until raccoon is tender,
2 to 3 hours, stirring once or twice.

## Cranberry Raccoon in Crockpot

Follow recipe above, using crockpot instead of
saucepan. Cover and cook on low heat until raccoon
is tender, 9 to 10 hours.

## ← Hasenpfeffer

*Marinating tenderizes hare or mature rabbits in this classic
German recipe. Serve with hot buttered egg noodles,
braised red cabbage, rye bread, and a good beer.*

 1 hare or 2 wild rabbits, cut up

MARINADE:
 2 cups red wine
 1 cup water
½ cup cider vinegar
 2 cloves garlic, minced
½ teaspoon dried thyme leaves
½ teaspoon dried rosemary leaves
½ teaspoon dried marjoram leaves
10 whole black peppercorns

½ cup all-purpose flour
 6 slices bacon, cut up
 8 ounces fresh mushrooms, cut into quarters
 1 cup chopped onion
 1 to 3 tablespoons butter
 1 teaspoon salt
½ cup dairy sour cream

4 to 6 servings

In large glass or ceramic mixing bowl, combine hare
pieces and all marinade ingredients. Cover bowl
with plastic wrap. Refrigerate for 2 or 3 days, turning hare pieces daily.

Lift hare pieces out of marinade. Pat dry with paper
towels; set aside. Strain and reserve 1½ cups marinade, discarding herbs and excess marinade. Place
flour on a sheet of waxed paper. Add hare pieces,
turning to coat. In Dutch oven, cook bacon over
medium heat until almost crisp. Add mushrooms
and onion. Cook until onion is tender, stirring
occasionally. Remove vegetable mixture with slotted spoon; set aside. Add 1 tablespoon butter to
pan. Add hare pieces. Brown on all sides, adding
additional butter if necessary. Return vegetable
mixture to Dutch oven. Add salt and reserved marinade. Heat to boiling. Reduce heat; cover. Simmer
until hare pieces are tender, 1 to 1¼ hours. With
slotted spoon, transfer hare pieces to heated serving
platter. Set aside and keep warm. Blend sour cream
into cooking liquid. Cook over medium heat until
heated through, stirring occasionally; do not boil.
Serve sauce over hare.

## Coonpfeffer

Follow recipe above, substituting 3 to 3½ pounds
raccoon pieces for the hare. Combine raccoon
pieces and marinade. Refrigerate for 3 to 4 days.
Continue as directed above, increasing cooking time
to 1½ to 2 hours.

## Raccoon with Sauerkraut →

1 tablespoon all-purpose flour
1 can (16 ounces) sauerkraut, rinsed and
    drained
1 large tart apple, cored and chopped
½ cup chicken broth
¼ cup packed brown sugar
½ teaspoon caraway seed
1 bay leaf
2 tablespoons Worcestershire sauce
½ teaspoon salt
½ teaspoon paprika
⅛ teaspoon pepper
3 to 4 pounds raccoon pieces, fat and
    glands removed
3 medium baking potatoes, cut in half

4 or 5 servings

Heat oven to 350°. Add flour to large (14 × 20-inch) oven cooking bag; shake to distribute. Place bag in 2-inch-deep roasting pan; set aside. In medium mixing bowl, combine sauerkraut, apple, chicken broth, brown sugar, and caraway seed; mix well. Spoon into cooking bag. Add bay leaf. In small bowl, combine Worcestershire sauce, salt, paprika, and pepper. Brush over raccoon pieces. Arrange raccoon pieces over sauerkraut mixture. Add potato halves. Close cooking bag with provided nylon tie. Make six ½-inch slits in top of bag. Bake until raccoon pieces are tender, 2 to 3 hours. Discard bay leaf before serving.

## Tuscan Hare with Pasta

*Hare is highly favored by Europeans. Many little restaurants in the Tuscany region of Italy serve hare sauce over pasta or polenta (cornmeal mush) during hunting season.*

1 hare, cut up
3 stalks celery, cut into 2-inch pieces
3 carrots, cut into 2-inch pieces
½ teaspoon dried rosemary leaves
1 bay leaf
10 whole black peppercorns
2 tablespoons red wine vinegar
3 cups dry red wine
2 cups water
⅓ cup olive oil
1 large onion, chopped
2 cloves garlic, minced
1 can (16 ounces) whole tomatoes, undrained
¼ cup tomato paste
2 teaspoons salt
    Hot cooked linguini or wide egg noodles
    Grated Parmesan cheese

4 to 6 servings

In Dutch oven, combine hare pieces, celery, carrots, rosemary, bay leaf, peppercorns, vinegar, wine, and water. Heat to boiling. Reduce heat; cover. Simmer for 45 minutes. Remove cover. Cook over medium heat for 1½ hours longer. Remove hare pieces; set aside to cool slightly. Strain cooking liquid into 2-cup measure; discard vegetables. If there is more than 1 cup cooking liquid, boil in medium saucepan until reduced to 1 cup. If there is less than 1 cup cooking liquid, add water to equal 1 cup. Set cooking liquid aside. Remove hare meat from bones; discard bones. Shred meat coarsely with fingers.

In Dutch oven, heat oil over medium heat. Add shredded meat. Cook, stirring frequently, until meat begins to brown, about 5 minutes. Scrape browned bits from bottom of pan. Add onion and garlic; cook 10 minutes longer. Add reserved cooking liquid, tomatoes and juice, tomato paste, and salt. Heat to boiling. Reduce heat to medium. Cook until moderately thick, 30 to 45 minutes, stirring occasionally. Serve sauce over hot linguini; sprinkle with grated Parmesan cheese.

## Coon Sauce Piquante

*To speed preparation of this spicy Southern dish, make the flour-and-oil roux while the raccoon pieces are in the pressure cooker.*

  4 to 5 pounds raccoon pieces, fat and
      glands removed

ROUX:
  3 tablespoons vegetable oil
  3 tablespoons all-purpose flour

VEGETABLE MIXTURE:
1½ cups chopped onion
  ⅔ cup chopped green pepper
  ¼ cup chopped celery
  ¼ cup snipped fresh parsley
  1 or 2 cloves garlic, minced

  1 can (28 ounces) whole tomatoes, cut up,
      juice reserved
  1 cup water
  1 teaspoon salt
  ¼ teaspoon cayenne pepper
      Hot cooked rice

6 to 8 servings

*How to Prepare Coon Sauce Piquante*

COOK raccoon pieces in pressure cooker as directed on page 89. Cool cooker as directed. Remove raccoon pieces from cooker; set aside to cool.

HEAT oil in large saucepan over medium heat. Stir in flour. Cook, stirring constantly, until dark golden brown, about 15 minutes.

STIR in vegetable mixture carefully. Stir in tomatoes and tomato juice, water, salt, and cayenne pepper. Heat to boiling. Reduce heat to medium-low. Cook, uncovered, until sauce thickens, about 1 hour.

REMOVE raccoon meat from bones while sauce cooks. Set meat aside; discard bones. When sauce is thickened, add raccoon meat to sauce. Cook until heated through, about 5 minutes. Serve over hot cooked rice.

## Florentine Rabbit Pasta ● VERY FAST ↑

*Northern Italian cooking often uses cream, rather than tomatoes, as the base for pasta sauces. In cooking language, Florentine usually means "with spinach." In this dish, the spinach is in the noodles.*

    2 tablespoons butter or margarine
    1 tablespoon minced fresh garlic
    2 cups shredded cooked wild rabbit
    2 cups whipping cream
    ¼ cup snipped fresh parsley
    1 teaspoon snipped fresh basil leaves or
        ½ teaspoon dried basil leaves
    ¼ teaspoon white pepper
    ⅛ teaspoon ground nutmeg
    1 package (12 to 16 ounces) spinach linguini
    ⅓ cup grated Parmesan cheese

                                              4 to 6 servings

In medium skillet, melt butter over medium heat. Add garlic. Cook and stir until tender but not brown. Add rabbit meat. Cook and stir until hot. Stir in cream, parsley, basil, pepper, and nutmeg. Cook over low heat until liquid is reduced by one-third, 10 to 15 minutes.

While rabbit mixture is cooking, cook linguini according to package directions. Drain. Set aside and keep warm. When rabbit mixture is reduced, remove from heat. Stir in Parmesan cheese. Serve over hot cooked noodles.

## Rabbit or Squirrel Salad

*One rabbit or two squirrels, cooked in the pressure cooker as directed on page 89, should provide enough meat for this salad. Boiled or leftover meat also works well.*

    2½ to 3 cups cubed cooked wild rabbit or
            squirrel
      1 medium onion, finely chopped
      4 hard-cooked eggs, chopped
      ½ cup mayonnaise or salad dressing
      ½ cup finely chopped celery
      ¼ cup finely chopped sweet pickles
      ¼ cup slivered almonds, optional
      3 tablespoons pickle juice
      ½ teaspoon salt
      ⅛ teaspoon pepper
        Lettuce leaves

                                              6 to 8 servings

In medium mixing bowl, combine all ingredients except lettuce leaves; mix well. Cover; chill at least 2 hours. To serve, line chilled individual plates or large serving bowl with lettuce leaves. Spoon rabbit mixture over leaves.

## Rabbit or Squirrel Pot Pie

Follow recipe on page 122 for Savory Pot Pie, substituting 2½ to 3 cups cut-up or shredded cooked rabbit or squirrel meat for the cooked turkey meat. Continue as directed.

# Upland Game Birds: Recipes

# Cooking Upland Game Birds

Wild upland birds differ somewhat from their domestic counterparts, so different cooking techniques are required. Wild birds, for one thing, have much less fat. You can roast a whole wild turkey much as you would a domestic one, but you must baste it more often to keep the meat moist. And wild birds have more flavor; the best recipes are those that do not cover up the natural taste.

Exactly how to cook an upland game bird depends on its size, its age, the color of its meat, and whether it was plucked or skinned.

Turkey, pheasant, grouse, and partridge can be roasted much like domestic birds of the same size. Medium-sized upland birds like pheasant, grouse, and partridge can also be split and grilled, or cut up and fried or braised. Small upland birds like quail, woodcock, and dove are often baked in a covered casserole with liquid to keep them moist. All upland birds are delicious when smoked (pages 149 to 152).

When dressing birds for the freezer, try to determine their age (page 32), then mark the packages accordingly. If the age is in doubt, it's best to cook with moist heat. Age is less important with small birds than with large ones.

On most upland birds, the breast meat is lighter in color than the leg or thigh meat. But on some, the breast is dark as well (see the chart below). Light meat dries out more quickly, and usually requires less cooking time than dark meat. By cutting birds up, you can cook each kind of meat exactly the right time. When packaging several birds for freezing, you may want to wrap the breasts and the legs in separate packages.

Plucked birds can be roasted whole or cut up and fried. The skin helps keep the meat moist during roasting, and when fried, it becomes crisp and tasty. Skinned birds are usually cut up and cooked with moist heat.

A wild turkey serves four to eight people, depending on its size. A pheasant serves two, and a pair of grouse serves three. Allow one partridge, two quail, or three woodcock or doves per person.

*Meat Color and Average Dressed Weight of Upland Birds*

| TYPE OF BIRD | BREAST | THIGHS/LEGS | AVERAGE DRESSED WEIGHT |
|---|---|---|---|
| Wild Turkey | White | Dark | 8 to 16 pounds |
| Sage Grouse | Dark | Very dark | 2 to 5 pounds |
| Ring-necked Pheasant | White | Dark | 1½ to 2¼ pounds |
| Sharp-tailed Grouse | Dark | Dark | 1¼ pounds |
| Ruffed Grouse | Very white | Medium | 1 pound |
| Chukar Partridge | White | Dark | 1 pound |
| Hungarian Partridge | Medium | Dark | ¾ pound |
| Mountain Quail | White | Dark | 7 ounces |
| Scaled Quail | White | Dark | 6 ounces |
| Bobwhite Quail | Medium | Medium | 6 ounces |
| Woodcock | Dark | Medium | 5 ounces |
| California Quail | White | Dark | 5 ounces |
| Gambel's Quail | White | Dark | 5 ounces |
| Mourning Dove | Dark | Dark | 4 ounces |

## Roasting Upland Game Birds

Birds with the skin on can be roasted in an open pan in a slow (325°) oven. Frequent basting helps keep the meat moist and makes the skin crisp and brown. Some cooks prefer roasting in oven cooking bags; the birds baste themselves, the skin browns well, and cleanup is easy.

Skinned birds should be handled differently. Moist cooking methods such as braising or steaming work better than open-pan roasting. If you choose to roast a skinned bird, cover the meat with strips of bacon, or rub it with softened butter and baste it frequently. Small birds like doves, quail, and woodcock can be wrapped in cabbage or grape leaves to retain moisture.

Only young birds should be roasted. Older, tougher ones should be cooked with moist heat.

Insert a standard meat thermometer into the thigh of a turkey or pheasant before roasting, or check near the end of the roasting time with an instant-reading meat thermometer. Birds are done when the thigh temperature reaches 185°. If roasting smaller birds, test for doneness by wiggling the leg. When it moves freely, the bird is done. You can also prick the thigh; the juices should run clear. Don't prick too often or it will lose too much juice.

## Roast Wild Turkey

*Oven cooking bags are excellent for roasting wild turkeys, since they keep the birds moist.*

1 tablespoon all-purpose flour
1 medium onion, sliced
3 stalks celery with leaves, chopped
1 wild turkey, skin on, thawed completely
    Salt and pepper
1 recipe Apricot Stuffing (page 142) or other
    dressing (optional)
    Melted butter or margarine
2 tablespoons all-purpose flour
3 tablespoons cold water

### Roasting Timetable for Wild Turkey

| TURKEY | WEIGHT BEFORE STUFFING | APPROXIMATE COOKING TIME* |
|---|---|---|
| Stuffed | 4 to 8 pounds | 2 to 2¾ hours |
| | 8 to 12 pounds | 2½ to 3 hours |
| | 12 to 15 pounds | 3 to 3½ hours |
| | 15 to 20 pounds | 3½ to 4 hours |
| | 20 to 25 pounds | 4½ to 5 hours |
| Unstuffed | 4 to 8 pounds | 1¾ to 2¼ hours |
| | 8 to 12 pounds | 2 to 2½ hours |
| | 12 to 15 pounds | 2½ to 3 hours |
| | 15 to 20 pounds | 3 to 3½ hours |
| | 20 to 25 pounds | 4 to 4½ hours |

\* Roast at 350° to an internal temperature of 185°

---

## *How to Roast a Wild Turkey in an Oven Cooking Bag*

ADD 1 tablespoon flour to turkey-size (19 × 23½-inch) oven cooking bag; shake to distribute. Place cooking bag in 13 × 9-inch roasting pan; add onion and celery. Heat oven to 350°.

SEASON cavity of bird with salt and pepper; stuff lightly with dressing. Place any extra dressing in buttered casserole; cover and refrigerate. You can also roast turkey unstuffed.

TRUSS the turkey by tying its legs together over the body cavity with kitchen string. To prevent the wings from drying out during roasting, tuck the tips under the turkey's back.

BRUSH entire turkey with melted butter; season with salt and pepper. Place turkey in oven cooking bag with onion and celery. Close bag with provided nylon tie.

INSERT meat thermometer into thigh through top of oven cooking bag. Make six ½-inch slits in top of bag. Roast according to chart. Bake extra dressing during the last 30 minutes.

REMOVE turkey from bag; wait 20 minutes before carving. For gravy: Blend 2 tablespoons flour into water. In saucepan, blend into drippings; cook over medium heat until thickened.

## Roast Pheasant with Sauerkraut

*The combination of sauerkraut and lingonberries makes this dish unusual, but delicious. Serve with crusty French bread and a good red wine.*

- 1 whole pheasant, skin on
- 2 tablespoons butter, softened
- 2 slices bacon, cut up
- 1 can (16 ounces) sauerkraut, rinsed and drained
- 1 cup pheasant stock (page 145) or chicken broth
- ¼ cup cognac or brandy
- 1 cup pheasant stock or chicken broth
- ⅓ cup canned lingonberries, rinsed*
- 3 tablespoons butter or margarine

2 or 3 servings

Heat oven to 375°. Rub softened butter over pheasant. Place in small roasting pan; cover. Roast until pheasant is tender and juices run clear when thigh is pricked, 35 to 45 minutes.

While pheasant is roasting, begin preparing remaining ingredients. In medium skillet, cook bacon over low heat until lightly browned. Add sauerkraut and 1 cup pheasant stock. Cook over medium heat until most of the liquid evaporates, 12 to 15 minutes. Remove from heat; set aside and keep warm.

When pheasant is done, transfer from roaster to heated platter; set aside and keep warm. Pour drippings from roaster into small bowl; set aside. In small saucepan, heat cognac gently over low heat until warm. Remove from heat; carefully ignite with a long match. When flame dies, add 1 cup pheasant stock and the lingonberries. Cook over high heat until the liquid is reduced by half, 10 to 15 minutes. Skim fat from reserved drippings. Add drippings and 3 tablespoons butter to lingonberry mixture; cook, stirring occasionally, until butter melts, about 2 minutes. Serve lingonberry sauce with pheasant and sauerkraut.

*\*Variation:* Substitute whole-berry cranberry sauce for lingonberries if you can't find lingonberries.

## Broiled Marinated Game Birds

Follow recipe at left, cooking in preheated broiler instead of over charcoal. Arrange birds on broiler rack, skin-side down. Place rack 4 to 6 inches from heat. Broil until done, 20 to 35 minutes, turning once and basting several times.

## Grilled Marinated Game Birds

- 2 whole pheasants or 4 whole partridge, skin on
- 1 recipe Lemon-Garlic Marinade (page 148) or other marinade
  Salt and freshly ground black pepper

4 servings

Split birds into halves with game shears (page 39). Place pheasant halves in large plastic food-storage bag. Pour prepared marinade over birds; seal bag. Refrigerate for at least 3 hours, or overnight, turning bag over occasionally.

Start charcoal briquets in grill. When briquets are covered with ash, spread them evenly in grill. Place grate above hot coals. Remove birds from marinade; reserve marinade. Arrange birds on grate, skin-side down. Grill until breasts are browned, 10 to 15 minutes, basting after every 5 minutes with reserved marinade. Turn birds over; continue grilling and basting until juices run clear when thigh is pricked. Remove from grill; season with salt and pepper.

## Sunday Roast Pheasant with Dressing →

*Serve this traditional roast with mashed potatoes and a green vegetable.*

- 1 whole pheasant, skin on*
- 1 recipe Onion-Bread Dressing (page 143) or other dressing
- 2 tablespoons butter or margarine, melted
- ½ cup pheasant stock (page 145) or chicken broth
- 3 tablespoons all-purpose flour
- ¼ cup milk
- 1 cup pheasant stock or chicken broth
  Salt and pepper

3 or 4 servings

Heat oven to 325°. Stuff pheasant lightly with prepared dressing. Place remaining dressing in greased 1-quart casserole; cover and refrigerate. Place pheasant, breast-side up, in small roaster; brush with melted butter. Add ½ cup pheasant stock to roaster. Cover; roast for 30 minutes, basting once. Place casserole with extra dressing in oven; cook pheasant and dressing 20 minutes longer. Uncover roaster; increase temperature to 350°. Continue roasting pheasant and dressing until pheasant is tender and juices run clear, and dressing is heated through, 20 to 30 minutes longer, basting pheasant once.

Transfer pheasant to heated platter; keep warm. In small bowl, blend flour and milk. Add 1 cup pheasant stock to juices in roaster; heat to simmering on stove top. Blend in flour mixture; cook over medium heat, stirring constantly, until thickened and bubbly. Add salt and pepper to taste. Serve gravy with pheasant and dressing.

*Variation:* If pheasant is skinned, do not brush with melted butter. Instead, dust stuffed pheasant lightly with 2 tablespoons flour; place 3 slices bacon over pheasant. Continue as directed.

## Sunday Roast Grouse with Dressing

Follow pheasant recipe above, substituting 2 sharptail or ruffed grouse for pheasant. Stuff grouse lightly; brush with melted butter. Place grouse, breast-side up, in small roaster; add ½ cup stock. Cover. Roast grouse and extra dressing for 30 minutes, basting grouse once. Uncover roaster; increase temperature to 350°. Continue roasting grouse and dressing until grouse are tender and juices run clear, and dressing is heated through, 20 to 30 minutes longer, basting grouse once. Continue as directed.

## Sunday Roast Partridge with Dressing

Follow pheasant recipe above, substituting 3 Hungarian or chukar partridge for pheasant. Stuff partridge lightly; brush with melted butter. Place partridge, breast-side up, in small roaster; add ½ cup stock. Cover; roast for 45 minutes, basting once. Place casserole with extra dressing in oven. Uncover roaster; increase temperature to 350°. Continue roasting partridge and dressing until partridge are tender and juices run clear, and dressing is heated through, 30 to 45 minutes longer, basting partridge once. Continue as directed.

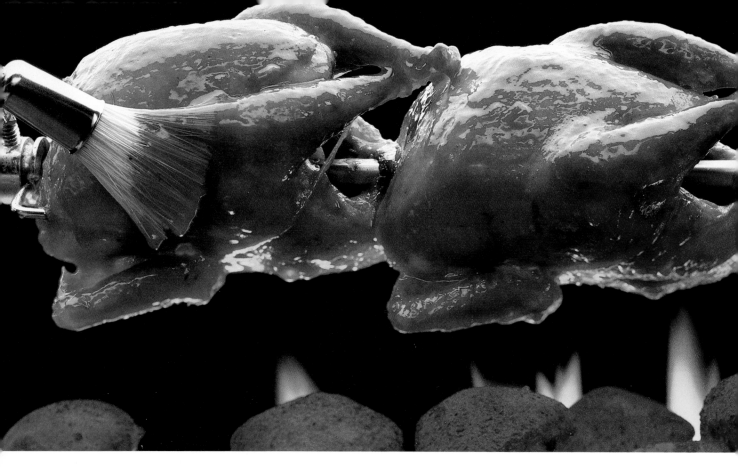

## Barbecued Partridge on Rotisserie ↑

½ cup hot pepper jelly
1 cup prepared barbecue sauce
2 to 4 whole partridge, skin on

2 to 4 servings

In small saucepan, cook hot pepper jelly and barbecue sauce over medium-low heat until sauce is hot and jelly melts, stirring constantly. Remove from heat; set aside and keep warm. Start charcoal briquets in rotisserie grill. Proceed as directed below.

TUCK wing tips behind each bird's back. Tie drumsticks with wet kitchen string. Bring string along thigh, then between wing and body. Tie string behind bird's back.

SKEWER birds on center of spit; secure with meat holders. If skewering three or four birds, you may skewer through ribs, changing direction of every other bird.

COOK skewered birds on rotisserie over prepared charcoal, brushing with sauce mixture after the first 20 minutes and then after every 10 minutes.

TEST for doneness by pricking thigh; juices will run clear when done. Reheat remaining sauce if necessary; serve with birds.

## Upland Birds in Oven Cooking Bag

1 tablespoon all-purpose flour
½ cup apple cider or orange juice
1 whole pheasant, or 2 grouse or partridge,
   skin on*
   Salt
3 tablespoons melted butter or margarine
¼ to ½ teaspoon bouquet garni seasoning or
   other herb mixture
½ apple

2 or 3 servings

Heat oven to 350°. Add flour to regular (10 × 16-inch) oven cooking bag; shake to distribute. Place bag in 10 × 6-inch baking dish. Pour cider into bag; stir with plastic or wooden spoon to blend into flour. Salt body cavity of pheasant. Brush outside of pheasant with melted butter; sprinkle with bouquet garni. Put ½ apple inside body cavity of pheasant (if cooking grouse or partridge, cut apple half into two pieces; place one piece inside cavity of each bird). Place pheasant in cooking bag. Close bag with provided nylon tie. Make six ½-inch slits in top of bag. Roast until juices run clear when thigh is pricked, 1 to 1¼ hours. Slit bag down center and fold back. Continue cooking until pheasant is brown, about 15 minutes. Remove and discard apple. Stir juices and spoon over pheasant, if desired.

*Variation:* If birds are skinned, cover with bacon strips if desired; omit butter. Use three bacon strips for a pheasant; two for each grouse or partridge.

## Vegetable Quail Casserole

1 large potato, peeled and cut into ¾-inch cubes
1 large carrot, grated
1 can (10¾ ounces) chicken broth or
   1¾ cups upland game bird stock (page 145)
4 to 6 whole quail, skin on
3 tablespoons all-purpose flour
¼ teaspoon salt
⅛ teaspoon pepper
¼ cup butter or margarine
½ teaspoon dried thyme leaves
¼ teaspoon dried rosemary leaves
¼ teaspoon dried marjoram leaves

2 or 3 servings

Heat oven to 350°. In medium saucepan, combine potato cubes, carrot, and chicken broth. Heat to boiling; reduce heat. Simmer 10 minutes. Remove from heat; set aside.

Split quail into halves with game shears (page 39). In large plastic food-storage bag, combine flour, salt, and pepper; shake to mix. Add quail; shake to coat. In medium skillet, melt butter over medium heat. Add quail; brown on both sides over medium-high heat. Arrange quail in 10-inch-square casserole. Pour vegetable and broth mixture over quail; sprinkle with thyme, rosemary, and marjoram. Cover casserole and bake until birds are tender, about 45 minutes.

## Savory Pineapple-Baked Quail ↑

8 whole quail, skin on
1 can (20 ounces) sliced pineapple, drained,
    juice reserved
2 teaspoons Worcestershire sauce
2 teaspoons Dijon-style mustard
1 teaspoon dried rosemary leaves
1 tablespoon cornstarch
1 small lemon, thinly sliced
   Salt and pepper

4 servings

Heat oven to 400°. Arrange quail, breast-side down, in 10-inch-square baking dish or 3-quart casserole; set aside. In small mixing bowl, blend pineapple juice, Worcestershire sauce, mustard, rosemary, and cornstarch. Pour pineapple-juice mixture over quail. Bake, uncovered, for 20 minutes. Turn quail breast-side up; arrange pineapple and lemon slices over quail. Baste with sauce. Bake until quail are tender and juices run clear, 15 to 30 minutes longer. Arrange quail and pineapple slices on platter. Strain sauce if desired; salt and pepper to taste. Serve over quail.

## Quail with Port Wine Sauce

4 to 6 whole quail, skin on
¼ cup all-purpose flour
½ teaspoon salt
2 tablespoons butter or margarine
¾ cup beef broth
¼ cup port wine
2 tablespoons raisins
3 whole cloves
1 tablespoon cornstarch
3 tablespoons cold water

2 or 3 servings

Split quail into halves with game shears (page 39). In large plastic food-storage bag, combine flour and salt; shake to mix. Add quail; shake to coat. In large skillet, melt butter over medium heat. Add quail; brown on both sides over medium-high heat. Add beef broth, port, raisins, and cloves to skillet. Heat to boiling. Reduce heat; cover. Simmer until quail are tender, 20 to 30 minutes. With slotted spoon, transfer quail to heated platter; set aside and keep warm. Remove cloves from skillet; discard.

In small mixing bowl, blend cornstarch and water. Blend into cooking liquid in skillet. Heat to boiling, stirring constantly. Cook, stirring constantly, until sauce is thickened and translucent. Serve over quail.

## Dove with Port Wine Sauce

Follow recipe above, substituting 8 to 12 doves. Decrease cooking time to 10 to 20 minutes.

## Quail Grilled in Cabbage Leaves

*This cooking method helps keep the birds moist. The recipe can easily be increased for an outdoor party.*

½ cup butter or margarine
 2 tablespoons snipped fresh parsley
¼ teaspoon dried thyme leaves
¼ teaspoon dried marjoram leaves
 6 whole quail, skin on
 6 large cabbage leaves*
   Salt

3 servings

*TIP: To loosen leaves from cabbage head, cut out core. Place cabbage in bowl; cover with cold water. Let stand about 10 minutes; remove leaves.

Cabbage leaves can also be loosened in a microwave: Core cabbage. Wrap in plastic wrap; place on plate. Microwave on High for 4 to 5 minutes, or until outer leaves are pliable.

*How to Prepare Quail Grilled in Cabbage Leaves*

MELT butter in small saucepan. Stir in parsley, thyme, and marjoram. Start charcoal briquets in grill.

BRUSH herb-butter mixture over outside of birds. Soak six 24-inch-long pieces of kitchen string in water.

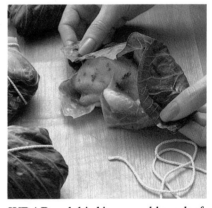

WRAP each bird in one cabbage leaf, folding ends of leaf in if leaves are large. Tie with wet string.

GRILL cabbage-wrapped birds over prepared charcoal for 15 minutes, turning frequently. Remove birds from grill. Carefully remove cabbage leaves; discard.

BRUSH quail with herb-butter mixture. Grill unwrapped birds until golden brown and cooked through, 3 to 5 minutes, turning once. Salt lightly before serving.

## Doves in Corn Bread Stuffing ↑

*Moist corn bread stuffing prevents the doves from becoming dry in this classic Southern recipe.*

STUFFING:
- ½ cup chopped celery
- ¼ cup sliced green onion
- 2 tablespoons snipped fresh parsley
- ¼ cup butter or margarine
- 3 cups corn bread stuffing mix
- 1 cup upland game bird stock (page 145) or chicken broth
- ½ teaspoon dried marjoram leaves
- ½ teaspoon salt
- ⅛ teaspoon pepper

- 8 dove breasts

4 servings

Heat oven to 350°. Lightly grease 2-quart casserole; set aside. In medium skillet, cook and stir celery, onion, and parsley in butter over medium heat until tender. Add remaining stuffing ingredients. Mix until moistened. Place half of stuffing mixture in prepared casserole. Arrange dove breasts over stuffing. Cover completely with remaining stuffing mixture. Bake, uncovered, until dove is cooked through and tender, about 1 hour.

## Quail in Corn Bread Stuffing

Follow recipe above, substituting 6 quail, split in half, for doves. Proceed as directed above.

## Hungarian Huns

*Buttered spaetzle or kluski noodles, rye bread, and green beans complete this meal.*

- 8 slices bacon, cut up
- ¾ cup all-purpose flour
- 1 tablespoon paprika
- 3 or 4 Hungarian partridge
- ¼ cup partridge stock (page 145) or chicken broth
- 3 tablespoons cider vinegar
- 1 small head green cabbage (about 1½ pounds), very coarsely chopped
- 1 medium onion, coarsely chopped
- 1 apple, cored and cut into ½-inch cubes
- ½ teaspoon caraway seed
- ½ teaspoon salt
- ⅛ teaspoon pepper

4 to 6 servings

In Dutch oven, cook bacon over medium heat until crisp, stirring frequently. Remove from heat. Remove bacon with slotted spoon; set aside. Reserve 3 tablespoons bacon fat in Dutch oven.

In large plastic food-storage bag, combine flour and paprika; shake to mix. Add one partridge; shake to coat. Repeat with remaining partridge. Add partridge to bacon fat in Dutch oven; brown on all sides over medium-high heat. Add reserved bacon and remaining ingredients to Dutch oven. Reduce heat; cover. Simmer until juices run clear when thigh is pricked, about 1 hour, rearranging birds and stirring vegetables once or twice.

## Stewed Partridge with Sage Dumplings →

STEWED PARTRIDGE:

   3 partridge, whole or cut up
1½ quarts water
   2 bay leaves
   1 teaspoon dried thyme leaves
   1 teaspoon dried rosemary leaves
   1 teaspoon dried summer savory leaves,
       optional
   2 teaspoons salt
 ⅛ teaspoon freshly ground black pepper
   4 carrots, cut into 1-inch chunks
   3 stalks celery, cut into 1-inch chunks
   2 medium onions, cut into wedges

SAGE DUMPLINGS:

1½ cups all-purpose flour
   2 teaspoons baking powder
 ½ teaspoon salt
 ½ to ¾ teaspoon crushed sage
 ⅔ cup milk
   3 tablespoons butter or margarine, melted

4 to 6 servings

In Dutch oven, combine partridge, water, bay leaves, thyme, rosemary, and savory. Heat to boiling. Reduce heat; cover. Simmer for 1½ hours. Add 2 teaspoons salt, the pepper, carrots, celery, and onions; cook until partridge and vegetables are tender, about 45 minutes. Remove from heat. Remove partridge and bay leaves from stock and vegetables; discard bay leaves. Cool partridge slightly.

Skim fat from broth. Remove partridge meat from bones and any skin. Tear meat into bite-size pieces and return to broth. Discard bones and skin.

To make dumplings, in medium mixing bowl, combine flour, baking powder, ½ teaspoon salt, and the sage; stir with fork to combine. Add milk and melted butter; stir until flour is moistened. Set aside.

Heat meat, vegetables, and broth until broth boils. Drop dumpling dough by heaping tablespoons onto broth mixture. Cook over medium-high heat for 5 minutes; cover and cook until dumplings are firm, about 10 minutes longer.

## Woodcock in Chablis  VERY FAST

*Serve this over toast points or rice as a brunch, light dinner, or hearty post-hunt breakfast.*

   6 to 8 woodcock breasts and legs, skinned
   3 tablespoons butter or margarine
   1 medium onion, thinly sliced
   1 cup sliced fresh mushrooms
   1 cup upland game bird stock (page 145) or
       chicken broth
 ½ cup chablis or dry white wine
   3 tablespoons all-purpose flour
 ½ teaspoon salt
       Dash pepper

2 to 4 servings

Bone woodcock breasts. Trim and discard any fat from breasts or legs. Discard fat and bones. In medium skillet, melt butter over medium heat. Add woodcock legs and boneless breast halves. Cook until woodcock has just lost its color. Remove woodcock from skillet with slotted spoon. Set aside.

Cook and stir onion in skillet over medium heat for 4 minutes. Add mushrooms. Cook and stir until vegetables are tender, 2 to 3 minutes. Return woodcock to skillet. In small bowl, blend remaining ingredients. Pour over woodcock and vegetables. Heat until bubbly, stirring constantly. Reduce heat; cover. Simmer until woodcock is tender, about 10 minutes, stirring once.

## Basque Pheasant ↑

*The Basque region is in the southern part of France, adjoining Spain; Basque cooking reflects both French and Spanish influence. Serve this dish with noodles or brown rice, and a spinach salad.*

 2 pheasants, cut up
⅓ cup packed brown sugar
¾ cup white wine
½ cup olive oil
½ cup vinegar
 1 cup pitted medium prunes
 1 cup pitted medium Spanish green olives
¼ cup capers with liquid
 3 cloves garlic, minced
 2 bay leaves
 2 tablespoons snipped fresh parsley
 2 tablespoons dried basil leaves

4 to 6 servings

In 13 × 9-inch baking dish, arrange pheasant pieces in single layer. In medium bowl, combine brown sugar, wine, oil, and vinegar; stir to mix. Add remaining ingredients. Stir to combine. Pour mixture over pheasant pieces; cover baking dish with plastic wrap. Refrigerate for at least 6 hours or overnight, turning pheasant pieces twice.

Heat oven to 350°. Remove plastic wrap from pan. Bake until pheasant is tender, about 1 hour, turning once. Transfer pheasant, olives, and prunes to platter with slotted spoon if desired.

## Pheasant in Creamy Mushroom Sauce

 1 can (10¾ ounces) condensed cream of
    mushroom soup
½ cup dairy sour cream
¼ cup milk
 2 tablespoons sherry, optional
½ cup all-purpose flour
 1 teaspoon salt
¼ teaspoon pepper
 2 pheasants, cut up
¼ cup vegetable oil
 8 ounces fresh whole mushrooms
 1 medium onion, cut into 8 chunks
¼ teaspoon dried thyme leaves, optional

4 to 6 servings

Heat oven to 300°. In small mixing bowl, blend soup, sour cream, milk, and sherry; set aside. In large plastic food-storage bag, combine flour, salt, and pepper; shake to mix. Add pheasant pieces; shake to coat. In Dutch oven, heat oil over medium-high heat. Add pheasant pieces; brown on all sides. Brown pieces in two batches if necessary. Return all pheasant to Dutch oven. Add mushrooms, onion, thyme, and reserved soup mixture. Cover. Bake until pheasant is tender, 1½ to 2 hours.

*Variation:* Follow recipe above, omitting the soup, sour cream, milk, and sherry. Reserve 3 tablespoons of seasoned flour after coating pheasant. After browning pheasant pieces, remove from Dutch oven. Remove Dutch oven from heat. Stir in reserved flour. Add 2 cups half-and-half. Cook over medium-low heat, stirring constantly, just until mixture bubbles. Return pheasant pieces to pan. Add mushrooms, onion, and thyme. Cover; bake as directed above.

## Pheasant with Apples

    3 tablespoons butter or margarine
    2 pheasants, cut up
    2 medium green apples, cored and cut into
        ½-inch slices
    1 cup sliced celery, ½ inch thick
    1 medium onion, finely chopped
    1 medium shallot, finely chopped
  ¾ cup dry white wine
1½ cups pheasant stock (page 145) or
        chicken broth
    2 tablespoons cornstarch
    2 tablespoons cold water
  ½ cup heavy cream
    1 tablespoon snipped fresh parsley
  ⅛ teaspoon salt
  ⅛ teaspoon pepper
    2 medium red apples
      Sugar
    3 tablespoons butter or margarine

4 to 6 servings

Heat oven to 350°. In Dutch oven, melt 3 table-spoons butter over medium heat. Add pheasant pieces; brown on all sides. Remove pheasant pieces with slotted spoon; set aside.

Add green apples, celery, onion, and shallot. Cook over medium-low heat until tender. Add wine and stock; cook over medium heat 5 minutes. Add pheasant pieces; remove from heat. Cover and bake until tender, about 40 minutes. Transfer pheasant to warm platter with tongs; set aside and keep warm.

Into small bowl, strain liquid from Dutch oven. Return strained liquid to Dutch oven; discard vegetables and apples in strainer. In small bowl, blend cornstarch and water; add to liquid in Dutch oven. Cook over medium heat, stirring constantly, until thickened and bubbly. Reduce heat to low. Add cream, parsley, salt and pepper; cook until hot. Set aside and keep warm.

Core red apples and cut into ½-inch slices. On waxed paper, sprinkle apples lightly with sugar. In medium skillet, melt 3 tablespoons butter over medium-low heat. Add apple slices; brown on both sides. Serve apples with pheasant; top with sauce.

## Baked Pheasant in Madeira ↑

1 pheasant, cut up
  Salt
¼ pound fresh mushrooms
1 tablespoon chopped onion or 1 teaspoon
    minced dried onion
1 cup pheasant stock (page 145) or
    chicken broth
1 cup Madeira wine
1 teaspoon lemon juice
1 tablespoon cornstarch
2 tablespoons cold water

2 or 3 servings

Heat oven to 325°. Sprinkle pheasant pieces lightly with salt; place in Dutch oven. Add mushrooms, onion, stock, wine, and lemon juice. Cover; bake until pheasant is tender, 1½ to 2½ hours. Transfer pheasant and mushrooms to heated platter with slotted spoon. Set aside and keep warm.

In small bowl, blend cornstarch and water. Blend into cooking liquid in Dutch oven. Heat to boiling, stirring constantly. Cook, stirring constantly, until thickened and translucent. Serve over pheasant.

## Pheasant in Madeira for Crockpot

Follow recipe above, except reduce Madeira to ½ cup. Place ingredients in crockpot instead of Dutch oven. Cover and cook on Low setting until tender, 7 to 8 hours. To make sauce, turn crockpot setting to High; heat liquid to boiling. Continue as directed.

## Smothered Birds

*The natural flavor of the bird comes through with this simple method. You may substitute 8 to 10 whole doves, 3 split partridge, 2 cut-up grouse, or 1 cut-up pheasant for the quail; adjust cooking times as indicated.*

6 quail, split into halves (page 39)
½ cup all-purpose flour
½ teaspoon salt
⅛ teaspoon pepper
¼ cup butter or margarine
1¼ cups upland game bird stock (page 145) or
    chicken broth, divided

2 or 3 servings

Pat quail halves dry. In large plastic food-storage bag, combine flour, salt, and pepper; shake to mix. Add quail halves; shake to coat. Remove quail pieces; set aside. Reserve 2 tablespoons flour mixture; discard remaining flour mixture.

In medium skillet, melt butter over medium heat. Add quail; brown on both sides. Add ¾ cup stock to skillet. Reduce heat; cover. Simmer until birds are tender, 35 to 45 minutes for quail or doves. Partridge or grouse will take 40 to 50 minutes; pheasant will take 50 to 60 minutes. Transfer quail halves to heated platter. Set aside and keep warm. In measuring cup or small bowl, blend reserved 2 tablespoons flour into remaining ½ cup stock. Blend into drippings in skillet. Cook over medium heat, stirring constantly, until thickened and bubbly. Serve gravy over birds.

## Deviled Birds

Follow recipe above, adding ¾ teaspoon dry mustard, ¾ teaspoon paprika, and ⅛ teaspoon cayenne pepper to ¾ cup stock. Continue as directed.

## Baked Smothered Pheasant

Follow recipe above, using 1 pheasant, cut up. Increase stock to 2 cups. Reserve 3 tablespoons flour mixture. Heat oven to 325°. After browning pheasant pieces, transfer to 3-quart casserole. Scatter one thinly-sliced onion over pheasant if desired. Stir reserved 3 tablespoons flour into drippings in skillet. Blend in 2 cups stock. Cook over medium heat, stirring constantly, until thickened and bubbly. Pour over pheasant pieces and onion. Cover casserole. Bake until pheasant is tender, 1 to 2 hours.

## Pheasant Paprika

*Prepare this dish with any pheasant pieces you have on hand — thighs, breasts, or a whole cut-up pheasant.*

   8   slices bacon, cut up
  ¼   cup chopped onion
 1½   cups instant mashed potato flakes
 1½   teaspoons paprika
 1½   teaspoons salt
   2   to 3 pounds pheasant pieces
  ¼   to ½ cup pheasant stock (page 145) or
         chicken broth
   2   tablespoons butter or margarine
   2   tablespoons all-purpose flour
   1   cup pheasant stock or chicken broth
  ⅔   cup milk
   1   tablespoon paprika
   1   to 1½ cups dairy sour cream
         Hot cooked egg noodles

4 to 6 servings

In medium skillet, cook bacon over medium heat until it just begins to brown. Add onion. Cook and stir until onion is tender. Remove from heat. With slotted spoon, remove bacon and onion from skillet. Set bacon and onion aside; reserve drippings.

In large plastic food-storage bag, combine potato flakes, 1½ teaspoons paprika, and salt; shake to mix. Add pheasant, a few pieces at a time, to bag; shake to coat. In reserved drippings, brown pheasant pieces over medium-high heat. Add ¼ cup stock to pan. Reduce heat; cover. Simmer until tender, 25 to 40 minutes, adding the additional ¼ cup stock to pan during cooking if necessary.

To prepare sauce: In 1-quart saucepan, melt butter over medium heat. Stir in flour. Blend in 1 cup stock. Cook, stirring constantly, until thickened and bubbly. Stir in milk, 1 tablespoon paprika, and reserved bacon and onion. Cook and stir until hot. Pour sauce over cooked pheasant in skillet. Cover and simmer 10 to 15 minutes. Remove from heat; skim fat. With slotted spoon, transfer pheasant to serving platter; keep warm. Stir sour cream into mixture in skillet. Cook over low heat until just heated; do not boil. Pour sauce over pheasant. Serve with hot cooked egg noodles.

## Stuffed Breasts of Grouse

*Ruffed grouse, sharp-tailed grouse, or young sage grouse can be used in this recipe. The number of servings can be increased easily. Simply allow two strips of bacon and one cupful of dressing for each grouse breast; each breast serves one.*

8  boneless breast halves from 4 grouse
8  slices bacon
1  recipe Onion-Bread Dressing (page 143)
3  tablespoons grouse stock (page 145) or chicken broth
1  recipe Easy Velouté Sauce or Dried Mushroom Sauce (page 147), optional

4 servings

### How to Prepare Stuffed Breasts of Grouse

PREPARE Onion-Bread Dressing as directed, adding additional 3 tablespoons stock. Heat oven to 350°.

PLACE one-fourth of the dressing on each of four breast halves. Top with remaining four breast halves.

WRAP 2 slices bacon around each breast-and-stuffing bundle. Secure bacon slices with toothpicks.

ARRANGE bacon-wrapped bundles in 8-inch-square baking dish. Cover baking dish with aluminum foil. Bake for 45 minutes.

REMOVE foil, and bake for 15 minutes longer. Transfer to serving platter or individual plates. Spoon Easy Velouté Sauce over each serving.

## Sharptail on Mushroom Toast  →

*Elegant fare for a small dinner party. This recipe works equally well with venison tenderloins.*

¼ cup dry red wine
¼ cup grouse stock (page 145) or chicken broth
1½ teaspoons all-purpose flour
¼ teaspoon dry mustard
¼ teaspoon salt
4 tablespoons butter or margarine
4 slices French bread, ¾ inch thick and
   5 to 6 inches across
1 tablespoon chopped shallot
1 tablespoon butter or margarine
8 ounces fresh mushrooms, very finely chopped
   Salt and freshly ground black pepper
1 tablespoon butter or margarine
1 tablespoon vegetable oil
4 boneless breast halves from 2 sharptail
   grouse
2 teaspoons snipped fresh parsley, optional

4 servings

In small bowl, blend wine, stock, flour, dry mustard, and ¼ teaspoon salt; set aside. In medium skillet, melt 2 tablespoons butter. Add 2 slices bread; turn quickly to coat both sides with melted butter. Cook over medium heat until golden brown on both sides. Repeat with remaining bread slices and 2 tablespoons butter; set aside and keep warm.

In medium skillet, cook and stir shallot in 1 tablespoon butter over medium heat until tender. Add chopped mushrooms. Cook over medium heat, stirring frequently, until the liquid has cooked off, about 10 minutes. Remove from heat. Salt and pepper to taste; set aside and keep warm.

In another medium skillet, melt remaining 1 tablespoon butter in oil over medium-low heat. Add breast halves. Cook over medium heat until well-browned on both sides but still moist in the center, about 10 minutes. Remove from skillet. Set aside and keep warm. Stir reserved wine mixture; blend into cooking juices in skillet. Cook and stir over medium heat until thickened and bubbly. Remove from heat; stir in parsley.

Spread each toast slice with one-fourth of the reserved mushroom mixture. Quickly slice each breast half into thin diagonal slices; arrange on mushroom toast. Drizzle about 2 tablespoons wine sauce over each portion.

## Sautéed Partridge Breast with Figs

*This dish can also be made with ruffed grouse. Serve with buttered new potatoes and fresh asparagus.*

6 dried figs, chopped
1 cup partridge stock (page 145) or chicken broth
1 tablespoon butter or margarine
4 boneless breast halves from 2 Chukar or
   Hungarian partridge
1 tablespoon balsamic vinegar*
¼ teaspoon dried thyme leaves
¼ cup butter, cut into 4 pieces
   Salt and freshly ground black pepper

2 servings

In small saucepan, heat figs and stock to boiling. Reduce heat; simmer until the stock thickens and darkens slightly, about 15 minutes. Remove from heat and set aside.

In medium skillet, melt 1 tablespoon butter over medium-low heat. Add breast halves. Cook until well-browned on both sides but still moist in the center, 6 to 10 minutes. Remove from skillet. Set aside and keep warm.

Wipe the skillet out with paper towels. Add the balsamic vinegar; swirl vinegar around skillet. Add the reserved fig mixture. Cook over high heat until the mixture is the consistency of heavy cream. Stir in thyme. Remove skillet from heat. Add butter, 1 tablespoon at a time, stirring well between each addition. Add salt and pepper to taste. Slice the reserved breasts; pour sauce over breasts.

*Balsamic vinegar is a robustly flavored, aged vinegar from Italy. Look for it at Italian specialty stores, or in specialty departments of large supermarkets.

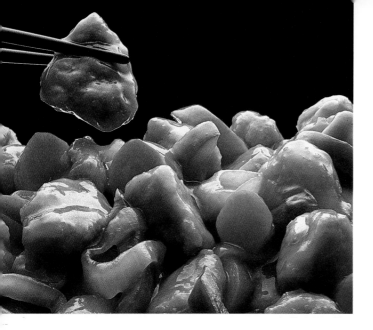

## Upland Stir-Fry  ↑

1 cup buttermilk baking mix
½ teaspoon pepper
¾ to 1 pound diced uncooked pheasant or other
   upland bird
2 eggs, slightly beaten
1 tablespoon peanut oil
3 medium carrots, cut diagonally into
   ½-inch pieces
1 green pepper, cut into strips
1 small onion, thinly sliced and separated
   into rings
2 tablespoons water
3 tablespoons peanut oil
¾ cup chicken broth
2 tablespoons teriyaki sauce
   Hot cooked rice

4 to 6 servings

In large plastic food-storage bag, combine baking mix and pepper; shake to mix. Set aside. In large mixing bowl, combine pheasant meat and eggs; stir to coat meat with egg. Remove pheasant from bowl with slotted spoon; transfer to plastic bag with baking mix. Shake to coat. Remove pheasant from bag; set aside. Discard excess baking mix and eggs.

In wok or large skillet, heat 1 tablespoon oil over medium-high heat until hot. Add carrots; cook and stir for about 2 minutes. Add green pepper and onion. Cook and stir for 1 minute longer. Add water; cover. Steam for 3 to 4 minutes, until vegetables are tender-crisp. Remove vegetables from wok and keep warm.

Add 3 tablespoons oil to wok; heat over medium-high heat until hot. Add pheasant; cook and stir until golden brown and no longer pink in center. Combine chicken broth and teriyaki sauce; pour over meat. Return vegetables to wok. Cook and stir until heated through. Serve with rice.

## Creamed Turkey Patties FAST

1 pound uncooked turkey, cut into
   1-inch pieces
1 cup whipping cream, divided
¼ cup all-purpose flour
¾ teaspoon salt, divided
¼ teaspoon pepper, divided
3 to 4 tablespoons butter or margarine
2 teaspoons all-purpose flour
1 tablespoon water
¼ cup white wine
2 tablespoons brandy
1½ cups sliced fresh mushrooms
   Dash ground nutmeg

6 servings

Heat oven to 175°. In food processor, combine turkey and ½ cup whipping cream. Process until smooth. With machine running, add remaining ½ cup whipping cream. Set aside. On waxed paper, combine ¼ cup flour, ½ teaspoon salt, and ⅛ teaspoon pepper; mix well. Divide turkey mixture into six equal portions. Drop each portion onto flour mixture. Shape into ½-inch-thick patty. In large skillet, melt 3 tablespoons butter over medium heat. Add half the turkey patties. Cook until center is firm, turning once. Transfer patties to heated platter; keep warm in oven. Add additional butter to skillet, if necessary. Repeat with remaining turkey patties.

In small bowl, blend 2 teaspoons flour into water; set aside. Slowly stir wine and brandy into skillet. Add mushrooms. Cook and stir over medium heat until just tender. Blend in ¼ teaspoon salt, ⅛ teaspoon pepper, dash nutmeg, and flour mixture. Cook over medium heat until thickened and bubbly, stirring constantly. Serve sauce over turkey patties.

*Variation:* Substitute boneless pheasant for turkey.

## Ruffed Grouse Strips in Butter ◆LOW-FAT VERY FAST

*This is the simplest way to fix grouse meat, and emphasizes the delicate, berry-like flavor. If you have more guests than grouse, this makes a lovely appetizer.*

1 grouse breast, skin and bones removed
2 tablespoons butter or margarine
   Salt and freshly ground black pepper

4 appetizer servings

Separate the *tenderloins,* which are thin fillets of meat on the inside of the breast, from the rest of the breast meat. Cut the breast halves lengthwise into ½-inch strips. In small skillet, melt butter over medium heat. Add grouse. Fry until golden brown and cooked through, about 5 minutes, turning occasionally. Salt and pepper to taste.

## Wild Turkey Picatta with Morels ↑

*In many states, spring turkey-hunting season coincides with the wild morel mushroom season. Hunters gather morels on their way to their hunting spots. This dish combines both of these special ingredients.*

    Half of wild turkey breast, skin and bones
      removed
 2  cups milk
 1  cup all-purpose flour
 ½  teaspoon salt
 ¼  teaspoon paprika
    Dash pepper
 4  to 6 tablespoons butter or margarine
 ¾  cup coarsely chopped fresh morels*
 3  tablespoons butter or margarine
 2  tablespoons coarsely chopped fresh chives
    Salt and freshly ground black pepper

4 or 5 servings

Cut turkey breast into ½-inch-thick slices across the grain. Place a slice on a cutting board between two sheets of waxed paper. Pound gently to ¼-inch thickness with saucer or flat side of meat mallet. Repeat with remaining slices. Place turkey slices in 12 × 8-inch baking dish. Add milk. Let stand at room temperature for 30 minutes. Remove turkey slices. Place milk in small bowl; set aside.

Heat oven to 175°. In large plastic food-storage bag, combine flour, salt, paprika, and pepper; shake to combine. Remove 3 tablespoons flour mixture; stir into reserved milk. Set aside. Add one turkey slice to remaining flour mixture in bag. Shake gently to coat. Remove and repeat with remaining slices. In medium skillet, melt 4 tablespoons butter over medium heat. Add half the turkey slices. Cook until golden brown and cooked through, turning once. Transfer turkey slices to heated platter; keep warm in oven. Add additional butter to skillet, if necessary. Repeat with remaining turkey slices.

In medium skillet, cook and stir mushrooms in 3 tablespoons butter over medium heat until tender. Stir in reserved milk mixture and chives. Cook over medium heat, stirring constantly, until thickened and bubbly. Salt and pepper to taste. If necessary, blend in additional milk to desired consistency. Serve sauce over turkey slices.

*\*Variation:* Substitute ½ ounce dried morels, available at specialty food stores, for fresh morels. Place dried morels in plastic bag. Add ¼ cup hot water. Squeeze out excess air; seal bag with tie. Set aside to rehydrate for about 15 minutes.

## Pheasant Picatta with Morels

Follow recipe above, substituting 2 or 3 whole pheasant breasts for half turkey breast. Cut breast halves from breast bone; remove skin. Save skin and bones for making stock. Cut breast halves in half across the width; pound to ⅜-inch thickness. Proceed as directed above.

## Savory Pot Pie

*Applesauce and a green salad complete this meal. This recipe also works well with cooked rabbit or squirrel.*

SINGLE PIE CRUST PASTRY:

   1  cup all-purpose flour
 1/4  teaspoon salt
 1/2  cup shortening
   2  to 4 tablespoons cold water

FILLING:

   2  tablespoons butter or margarine
 1/2  cup water
   1  cup thinly sliced carrot
   1  medium potato, cut into 1/4-inch cubes
 1/2  cup thinly sliced celery
 1/2  cup chopped onion
 1/2  cup frozen peas
2 1/2  to 3 cups cut-up cooked turkey, pheasant
     or partridge
   1  recipe Dried Mushroom Sauce or Easy
     Velouté Sauce (page 147)
   1  egg yolk, slightly beaten

4 to 6 servings

Heat oven to 375°. To prepare pastry: In medium mixing bowl, combine flour and salt. Cut shortening into flour until particles resemble coarse crumbs or small peas. Sprinkle with cold water while tossing with fork, until particles are just moist enough to cling together. Shape into a ball. Wrap with plastic wrap and refrigerate.

In medium saucepan, combine butter and water. Heat until butter melts. Add carrot; cover and cook over medium heat for 3 minutes. Add potato; re-cover and cook for 5 minutes longer, stirring twice. Add celery, onion, and peas; re-cover and cook for 3 minutes, stirring once. Drain vegetable mixture. In medium mixing bowl, combine vegetable mixture, cooked meat, and prepared sauce. Stir well to mix. Transfer mixture to 1 1/2-quart casserole.

On lightly floured surface, roll out pastry slightly larger than top of casserole. Place pastry on top of casserole. Turn edge of pastry under; flute edge if desired. Brush pastry with beaten egg yolk. Cut a small hole in center of pastry to allow steam to escape. Bake until golden brown, 30 to 35 minutes.

## Oriental Pheasant Salad  →

*Served with hot biscuits and chilled white wine or iced tea, this makes a refreshing light lunch.*

    2  cups cut-up cooked pheasant or grouse
    1  cup seedless green grapes
    1  can (8 ounces) pineapple chunks, drained
    1  can (8 ounces) sliced water chestnuts, drained
    ½  cup diagonally sliced celery
    1  apple, cored and cut into ½-inch cubes
    1  tablespoon fresh lemon juice
    ¼  cup mayonnaise or salad dressing
    ¼  cup dairy sour cream
    1  teaspoon prepared mustard
       Lettuce leaves
    ½  cup chow mein noodles

4 to 6 servings

In large bowl, combine pheasant, grapes, pineapple chunks, water chestnuts, and celery. In small mixing bowl, toss apple cubes with lemon juice; add to pheasant mixture. In same small mixing bowl, blend mayonnaise, sour cream, and mustard; pour over pheasant mixture. Mix well; refrigerate at least 2 hours to blend flavors. To serve, line chilled individual plates or large serving bowl with lettuce leaves; spoon pheasant mixture over leaves. Top with chow mein noodles.

## Turkey and Dressing Casserole

*Leftover cooked pheasant also works well for this recipe.*

    3  cups cut-up cooked turkey
    5 to 6 cups unseasoned croutons
    3  tablespoons finely chopped onion
    ¼  cup finely chopped carrot
    ¼  cup finely chopped celery
    ½  cup butter or margarine
    ½  cup cream or evaporated milk
    2  cups turkey stock (page 145) or
       chicken broth
 1¼  teaspoons poultry seasoning
    ¾  teaspoon salt
    ⅛  teaspoon pepper

6 to 8 servings

Heat oven to 350°. Grease 3-quart casserole; set aside. In large mixing bowl, combine turkey and croutons; set aside. In medium saucepan, combine remaining ingredients. Cook over medium heat until butter melts, stirring occasionally. Pour mixture over turkey and croutons. Toss lightly to mix. Place in prepared casserole; cover. Bake for 30 minutes; increase oven temperature to 375°. Uncover casserole and bake for 10 minutes longer.

## Turkey Lentil Soup ◆ LOW-FAT

*Use the leftover carcass from your roast turkey to make this interesting soup.*

     1 turkey carcass, fairly meaty
     8 cups water
     1 medium onion, quartered
    ¼ cup snipped fresh parsley
     1 clove garlic, minced
     2 teaspoons salt
    ¼ teaspoon dried marjoram leaves
    ¼ teaspoon pepper
    ⅛ teaspoon dried thyme leaves
     1 cup thinly sliced carrot
    ¾ cup dried lentils
    ½ cup thinly sliced celery
    ½ teaspoon salt
       Dash pepper

                                    2 quarts

In Dutch oven, combine turkey carcass (cut up if desired), water, onion, parsley, garlic, 2 teaspoons salt, marjoram, ¼ teaspoon pepper, and thyme. Heat to boiling. Reduce heat; cover. Simmer until meat on bones is very tender, 1½ to 2 hours. Strain broth through several layers of cheesecloth; reserve broth. Remove meat from carcass; discard carcass and any skin. Return broth and meat to Dutch oven. Stir in remaining ingredients. Heat to boiling. Reduce heat; cover. Simmer until lentils are tender, about 30 minutes.

## Birds in Aspic ◆ LOW-FAT

*Use leftover meat from any upland bird in this recipe; leftover rabbit or squirrel also works well. Serve with seasoned mayonnaise and a mustard sauce.*

     1 large or several smaller carcasses from cooked
         upland birds
     1 small onion, sliced
     2 celery stalks, cut in thirds
     1 bay leaf
     1 teaspoon salt
       Hot water
     3 tablespoons white vinegar
     3 tablespoons dry white wine or sauterne
     2 teaspoons unflavored gelatin
     2 tablespoons cold water
     4 cups cut-up cooked turkey or other upland
         game bird
       Radishes and parsley for garnish, optional

                                    6 to 8 servings

Cut or break carcasses into pieces; place in 6-quart saucepan. Add onion, celery, bay leaf, and salt. Add hot water to cover bones. Heat to boiling. Reduce heat; simmer for 2½ hours. Remove and discard bones and vegetables. Strain broth through several layers of cheesecloth. Skim fat from surface. Reserve 1½ cups stock; refrigerate or freeze remaining stock for use in other recipes.

In small saucepan, combine 1½ cups reserved stock, vinegar, and wine. Heat to boiling; cook until liquid is reduced to 1 cup. Reduce heat to low; cover. In small bowl, sprinkle gelatin over cold water; let stand 5 minutes to soften. Add gelatin to hot stock. Cook over medium-high heat until gelatin dissolves, stirring constantly. Remove from heat.

In 6-cup mold, arrange meat, alternating dark meat with light meat if desired. Pack firmly. Pour stock mixture evenly over meat. Chill until firm, at least 3 hours. To serve, dip mold briefly into warm water; place serving plate on top of mold and invert mold and plate together, holding firmly. Garnish with radishes and parsley.

## Partridge Newburg  VERY FAST ↑

¾ cup half-and-half
¾ cup milk
1 envelope (.86 ounce) chicken gravy mix
8 ounces fresh mushrooms, sliced
¼ cup butter or margarine
¼ teaspoon seasoned salt
¼ teaspoon curry powder
⅛ teaspoon white pepper
2 egg yolks, slightly beaten
1½ to 2 cups cut-up cooked partridge
2 tablespoons cream sherry
1 tablespoon diced pimiento, drained
Baked patty shells or hot buttered toast points

4 to 6 servings

In small mixing bowl, blend half-and-half, milk, and gravy mix; set aside. In medium skillet, cook and stir mushrooms in butter until just tender. Stir in gravy mixture, seasoned salt, curry powder, and white pepper. Cook over medium heat, stirring constantly, until thickened and bubbly. Remove from heat. Stir a small amount of hot mixture into egg yolks. Stir back into mixture in skillet. Cook over medium-low heat, stirring constantly, until very hot. Stir in partridge, sherry, and pimiento. Cook over medium-low heat, stirring constantly, until heated through. Serve in patty shells.

## Creamy Rice Casserole FAST

⅓ cup sliced celery
⅓ cup chopped onion
¼ cup chopped carrot
2 tablespoons butter or margarine
2 cups cut-up cooked turkey or other upland game bird
2 cups cooked rice (wild, brown, white, or mixed)
1 can (10¾ ounces) condensed cream of mushroom soup
½ cup milk
¼ teaspoon salt
⅛ teaspoon dried thyme leaves
⅛ teaspoon pepper

4 to 6 servings

Heat oven to 375°. Lightly grease a 2-quart casserole; set aside. In medium skillet, cook and stir celery, onion, and carrot in butter over medium heat until tender. Transfer vegetable mixture to prepared casserole. Add remaining ingredients. Mix well; cover. Bake until casserole is hot and bubbly, about 30 minutes.

# Cooking Waterfowl

For many lucky families, roast wild goose is the traditional holiday fare. Dedicated waterfowlers think nothing of setting out hours before dawn, then waiting in the cold and damp for a chance at a magnificent Canada goose to grace the Thanksgiving or Christmas table.

Wild geese and ducks are more robustly flavored than domestic waterfowl. They're delicious if properly prepared, although the dark, rich meat is not to everyone's liking. Geese have a milder flavor than ducks, and may be a better choice for serving to those who have never tasted wild waterfowl.

The taste of ducks varies greatly, depending on the species and the individual duck. Canvasbacks, ringnecks, mallards, and teal are the favorites for eating. Redheads, black ducks, wood ducks, and pintails also are excellent. But a duck's diet affects the taste, so there's some variation within any species.

Smell the meat before cooking it. If it has a muddy or fishy odor, you may wish to marinate it or cook it with a flavorful sauce.

Next, consider the fat content of each duck you take. One that's just begun its winter migration will have more fat than one that's recently flown a long distance. As ducks recuperate from migration, they begin to build up fat again. One taken on its wintering area in the late season will be plumper than one taken earlier.

The breast is the best place to check for fat. If you can see a yellow layer through the skin, the duck is fat enough for roasting. Another option is smoking (pages 151, 152). Scaup, ringnecks, goldeneyes, and other diving ducks are especially good for this, since they usually have more fat than mallards, teal, wood ducks, and other *puddle ducks*. If the duck's breast skin appears dark, however, it may lack fat. Lean ducks require more basting, or moist cooking.

Also, consider the bird's age (page 32). Old, tough birds can be tenderized by long, moist cooking, by parboiling and then roasting, or by pressure-cooking. To pressure-cook, first remove the skin and excess fat. Cut a large bird into pieces to fit the cooker; smaller birds can be cooked whole. Follow the directions on page 89, cooking 20 to 25 minutes at 15 pounds pressure. The pressure-cooked meat is excellent in casseroles and salads.

Some people enjoy their duck cooked rare. The meat is juicy and flavorful, slightly reminiscent of rare beef. At the other extreme, some prefer it cooked at low heat until the meat literally falls off the bone.

To determine degree of doneness, prick the bird with a fork. If the juices are rosy, the bird is rare. The meat will be slightly springy to the touch; internal temperature will be 145° to 150°. Well-done birds read 180°; juices will run clear. The drumstick should wiggle freely in the joint.

Larger ducks, such as mallards, canvasbacks, black ducks, and redheads, will serve two people each. Gadwalls, widgeons, wood ducks, pintails, ringnecks, scaups, and goldeneyes are smaller; three ducks will serve four. Allow one teal per person. A Canada goose will serve from three to eight people, depending on its size. Blue geese, snow geese, and white-fronted geese are smaller than most Canadas, and usually serve two to six each.

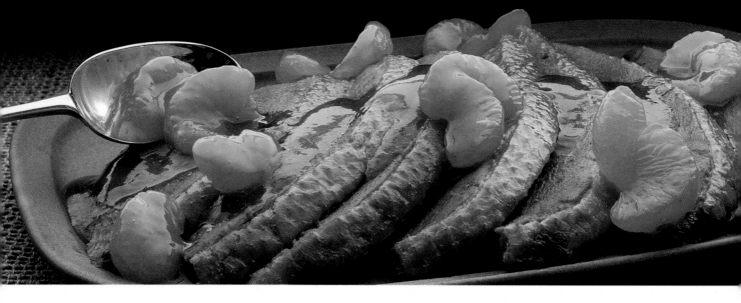

## Mandarin Goose ↑

- 1 whole wild goose, 3 to 6 pounds, skin on
  Salt
- 1 medium onion, cut in half
- 1 tablespoon all-purpose flour
- ½ cup port wine
- ¼ cup orange juice
- 1 tablespoon lemon juice
- ½ teaspoon dry mustard
- ¼ cup currant jelly
- 2 tablespoons cornstarch
- 2 tablespoons cold water
- 1 can (11 ounces) mandarin orange segments, drained

3 to 6 servings

Heat oven to 350°. Sprinkle cavity and outside of goose lightly with salt; place onion in cavity. Add flour to large or turkey-sized oven cooking bag; shake to distribute. Place bag in roasting pan. In small bowl, blend wine, orange juice, lemon juice, and dry mustard. Add to cooking bag; stir with plastic or wooden spoon to blend into flour. Place goose, breast-side up, in cooking bag. Close cooking bag with provided nylon tie; make six ½-inch slits in top of bag. Roast until almost desired doneness, 15 to 20 minutes per pound. Slit cooking bag down center. Roast until goose is brown, 15 to 20 minutes longer. Remove goose from bag; discard onion. Keep goose warm.

Strain juices from cooking bag into 4-cup measure. Skim fat. Add water if necessary to equal 2 cups. In medium saucepan, combine juices and jelly. Cook over medium heat, stirring constantly, until jelly melts. In small bowl, blend cornstarch and water. Stir into jelly mixture. Cook over medium heat, stirring constantly, until thickened and bubbly. Add mandarin orange segments to gravy; heat through. Serve gravy with goose.

## Stuffed Roast Goose

*Prepare a young goose with this traditional recipe.*

- 1 whole wild Canada goose, 3 to 5 pounds, skin on
  Salt and pepper
- 1 recipe Apricot Stuffing (page 142) or other dressing

3 to 5 servings

Heat oven to 400°. Sprinkle cavity of goose lightly with salt and pepper. Stuff lightly with Apricot Stuffing. Tuck wing tips behind back. Tie drumsticks across cavity. Place goose, breast-side up, on rack in roasting pan. Sprinkle lightly with salt and pepper. Roast for 1 hour, basting with pan juices frequently. Drain and discard excess fat during roasting. Reduce oven temperature to 325°. Roast until goose is desired doneness, 1 to 1½ hours longer, basting frequently.

## "Poached" Wild Goose

*Although this recipe may sound illegal, the title refers to the cooking technique, not the method of procurement! Use this recipe if you have a mature goose to cook.*

- 1 whole wild goose, skin on
- 1 large onion, quartered
- 2 stalks celery, cut into 1-inch pieces
- 2 carrots, cut into 1-inch pieces
- 1 bay leaf
  Hot water
- 2 tablespoons butter or margarine, melted

4 to 8 servings

In large stockpot, combine goose, onion, celery, carrots, and bay leaf. Add water to cover. Heat to boiling. Reduce heat. Simmer until tender, 1½ to 2½ hours; if size of goose prohibits covering with water, turn goose over once or twice during cooking. Heat oven to 400°. Drain goose; strain broth and save for other recipes. Pat goose dry. Place in roasting pan. Brush with melted butter. Roast until skin is brown and crisp, 20 to 30 minutes.

## Roast Goose with Baked Apples

*This beautiful presentation would be perfect for a holiday meal. Serve with green vegetables and freshly baked bread.*

BAKED APPLES:

 6 to 8 firm medium apples, cored
 1 cup mashed cooked sweet potatoes
 ¼ cup packed brown sugar
 2 tablespoons butter or margarine, melted
 ¼ teaspoon salt
    Dash pepper

 1 whole wild goose, 6 to 8 pounds, skin on
    Seasoned salt
    Salt and pepper
 1 carrot, cut into 1-inch pieces
 1 stalk celery, cut into 1-inch pieces
 1 medium onion, cut into 8 pieces
    Apple brandy or Calvados, optional

6 to 8 servings

### How to Prepare Roast Goose with Baked Apples

REMOVE a thin strip of peel from the top of each apple. In medium mixing bowl, combine remaining apple ingredients. Mix well.

STUFF apples with sweet potato mixture, mounding on top. Place in shallow baking dish. Set apples aside. Heat oven to 325°.

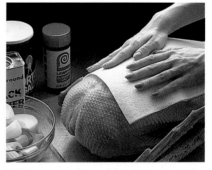

PAT goose dry with paper towels. Sprinkle cavity lightly with seasoned salt, salt, and pepper. Place carrot, celery, and onion in cavity.

TIE drumsticks across cavity. Tuck wing tips behind back. Place, breast-side up, on rack in roasting pan. Sprinkle outside of goose with seasoned salt, salt, and pepper.

ROAST, basting frequently with pan juices and sprinkling occasionally with brandy, until desired doneness, 20 to 25 minutes per pound. Drain and discard excess fat during roasting.

PLACE stuffed apples in oven during last 30 to 45 minutes of roasting. Baste apples frequently with goose drippings. Remove apples when fork-tender; serve with goose.

## Blue Goose with Cherries

*This recipe can also be used for a large duck, like a canvasback or mallard, or for two smaller ducks.*

2 to 3-pound blue goose, skin on or skinned
1 can (16 ounces) pitted dark sweet cherries
1 tablespoon butter or margarine
1 tablespoon vegetable oil
1 small onion, chopped
1 tablespoon all-purpose flour
½ cup water
2 tablespoons cream sherry
1 tablespoon packed brown sugar
1 teaspoon instant beef bouillon granules
½ teaspoon ground cinnamon
¼ teaspoon salt
2 tablespoons cold water, optional
1 to 2 tablespoons cornstarch, optional

2 or 3 servings

Split goose into halves (page 39), removing backbone. Cut each half into two pieces, cutting at a right angle to the first cuts.* Set aside. Drain cherries, reserving ½ cup juice. Set aside. In Dutch oven, melt butter in oil over medium heat. Add onion. Cook and stir until tender. Add goose pieces; brown lightly on all sides. Remove goose pieces; set aside.

Stir flour into onion mixture. Stir in reserved cherry juice, ½ cup water, sherry, brown sugar, bouillon granules, cinnamon, and salt. Add goose pieces and cherries. Heat to boiling. Reduce heat; cover. Simmer until goose pieces are tender, 1½ to 2 hours, turning pieces once. Transfer goose to heated serving platter. Set aside and keep warm. Skim sauce. If sauce is thinner than desired, blend 2 tablespoons water with the cornstarch. Stir into sauce. Cook over medium heat, stirring constantly, until thickened and translucent. Serve sauce over goose pieces.

*\*Variation:* Instead of quartering the goose as described above, portion as pictured on page 40.

## Blue Goose with Cherries for Crockpot

Follow recipe above, except transfer browned goose pieces to crockpot. Stir flour into onion mixture. Omit ½ cup water. Stir in reserved cherry juice, sherry, brown sugar, bouillon granules, cinnamon, and salt. Cook, stirring constantly, until thickened. Stir in cherries. Pour over goose pieces in crockpot. Cover; cook on low heat until tender, 6 to 7 hours. Transfer goose pieces to heated serving platter. Set aside and keep warm. Skim sauce. If sauce is thinner than desired, blend 2 tablespoons water with cornstarch. Stir into sauce. Increase heat setting to high. Cook, stirring constantly, until thickened and translucent. Serve sauce over goose pieces.

## Limerick Goose with Potatoes

*Potatoes and ground pork combine for the stuffing in this Irish-inspired recipe.*

2 quarts water
1 teaspoon salt
6 medium white potatoes (about 3 pounds), peeled and quartered
½ pound lean ground pork
1 tablespoon butter or margarine
¾ cup chopped onion
⅔ cup chopped celery
1 teaspoon poultry seasoning
1 teaspoon salt
¼ teaspoon pepper
3 cups cubed stale bread
¼ cup snipped fresh parsley or
    1 tablespoon dried parsley flakes
1 whole wild goose, skin on
    Salt and pepper

4 to 8 servings

In Dutch oven, heat water and 1 teaspoon salt to boiling. Add potatoes. Return to boiling. Reduce heat; cover. Simmer until potatoes are fork-tender, 25 to 35 minutes. Drain, reserving cooking liquid. In large mixing bowl, mash potatoes, or rice with a potato ricer. Heat oven to 375°.

In medium skillet, cook pork over medium heat until brown, stirring occasionally. Remove with slotted spoon and add to potatoes. Reserve 1 tablespoon drippings in skillet; discard remaining drippings. Add butter to reserved drippings; melt over medium heat. Add onion and celery. Cook and stir until vegetables are tender. Remove from heat. Stir in poultry seasoning, 1 teaspoon salt, and ¼ teaspoon pepper. Add onion mixture, bread cubes, and parsley to potatoes; mix well. Set aside.

Sprinkle cavity of goose lightly with salt and pepper. Stuff loosely with potato mixture. Place any remaining stuffing in buttered casserole; cover and set aside. Tuck wing tips behind back. Tie drumsticks across cavity. Place goose, breast-side up, on rack in roasting pan. Roast, basting frequently with reserved potato water, until desired doneness, 20 to 25 minutes per pound. Bake extra stuffing during last half hour of roasting.

## Danish Pickled Duck ▸LOW-FAT ↑

*Surprise your guests with this delicious and unusual appetizer. The duck meat becomes flaky and sweet, a bit like mild tuna fish. Serve with crackers, and pickled beets for color.*

2 whole wild ducks, skin on
    Cold water
    Salt
5 bay leaves
1 clove garlic, quartered
1 teaspoon ground allspice
10 whole juniper berries
8 whole black peppercorns
1½ cups red wine

10 to 12 appetizer servings

Place ducks in Dutch oven or stockpot. Add a measured amount of water, enough to just cover ducks. Add 1 tablespoon salt for each quart of water used. Add remaining ingredients. Heat to boiling. Reduce heat; cover. Simmer until tender, 2½ to 3½ hours. Remove from heat. Transfer ducks and liquid to large glass casserole or mixing bowl. Cool ducks and liquid. Cover and refrigerate for 3 days, turning ducks once or twice. To serve, skin and remove meat from bones. Discard skin and bones.

TIP: Substitute leftover pickled duck for the cooked rabbit in Rabbit Salad, page 99; or for tuna fish in your favorite tuna salad recipe. Pickled duck is also excellent in a chef's salad.

## Northwoods Duck and Wild Rice

*Wild rice is actually the seed of an aquatic grass that is abundant in the North. In this recipe, the rice is not boiled in the usual manner, but soaked and then cooked inside the ducks. The rice is delightfully nutty and crunchy as a result.*

 1 cup wild rice, rinsed
   Cold water
¼ cup butter
   Seasoned salt
   Pepper
 3 or 4 whole wood ducks or other medium
   ducks, skin on
 1 cup dry white wine

4 or 5 servings

Place wild rice in medium mixing bowl. Cover with water. Soak at room temperature for at least 8 hours or overnight. Drain wild rice thoroughly. Spread on double layer of paper towels; pat dry. Return wild rice to mixing bowl. In small saucepan, melt butter over medium-low heat. Stir in seasoned salt and pepper to taste. Pour melted butter over wild rice; mix well. Set aside.

Heat oven to 425°. Tuck ducks' wing tips behind backs. Stuff ducks very lightly with wild rice mixture. Tie drumsticks across cavity. Place ducks on rack in roasting pan. Sprinkle lightly with seasoned salt and pepper. Roast for 30 minutes. Drain and discard excess fat. Add wine to roasting pan; cover. Reduce oven temperature to 350°. Roast ducks until tender, 1 to 2 hours longer, basting with pan juices after every 15 minutes. If desired, roast uncovered for last 30 minutes.

## ← Polynesian Roast Duck

*When you're expecting company, this is a good recipe to prepare. Follow the serving suggestion at the bottom of the recipe, then set the platter out on a buffet table.*

 4 mallards or other large wild ducks, or
   6 to 8 smaller wild ducks, skin on or skinned
 2 quarts water
¾ pound mild pork sausage
 1 cup chopped green pepper
¾ cup chopped celery
⅓ cup chopped onion
 4 cups cooked white, brown, or mixed rice
 1 can (20 ounces) crushed pineapple, drained
½ teaspoon salt
¼ teaspoon pepper
¼ cup packed brown sugar
¼ cup white wine

SAUCE:
 3 tablespoons cider vinegar
 2 tablespoons cornstarch
1½ cups fresh orange juice
¼ cup granulated sugar
½ teaspoon salt
   Dash pepper

8 servings

In Dutch oven, combine ducks and water. Heat to boiling. Reduce heat. Simmer 45 minutes for large ducks, 30 minutes for smaller ducks. Drain, reserving broth. Set ducks aside. Skim fat and strain broth. Reserve 1 cup broth for sauce. Save remaining broth for use in other recipes.

Heat oven to 350°. Grease a 13 × 9-inch baking pan; set aside. In large skillet, cook and stir sausage, green pepper, celery, and onion over medium heat until sausage is brown and vegetables are tender. Drain. In large mixing bowl, combine sausage mixture, rice, pineapple, salt, and pepper. Mix well. Stuff ducks lightly. Spoon remaining rice mixture into baking pan. Arrange ducks on rice. In small saucepan, combine brown sugar and wine. Heat to boiling, stirring occasionally. Brush ducks with wine mixture. Bake until ducks are deep golden brown, about 1¼ hours for large ducks, 45 minutes for smaller ducks, brushing with wine mixture occasionally.

While ducks are baking, prepare sauce. In medium saucepan, blend vinegar and cornstarch. Blend in reserved broth and remaining sauce ingredients. Heat to boiling over medium-high heat, stirring constantly. Boil 1 minute. Serve sauce with ducks and rice.

*Serving Suggestion:* If desired, set cooked ducks aside to cool slightly. Remove rice stuffing from ducks; add to rice mixture in baking pan, or combine on serving platter. Slice breast and thigh meat from ducks. Arrange over rice mixture.

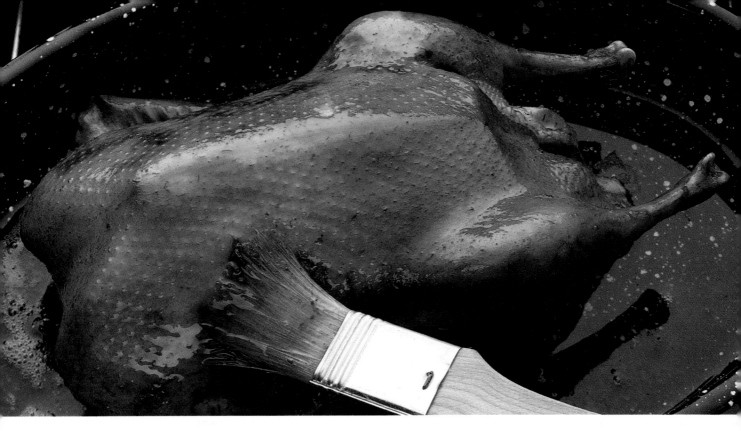

## Roast Lemon-Mint Duck ↑

 1  whole mallard or other large wild duck,
       skin on
 1  tablespoon finely chopped fresh mint
      Grated rind and juice from one small lemon
 3  tablespoons softened butter, divided
 ¼  teaspoon pepper
 ⅛  teaspoon salt
 1  cup duck stock (page 145) or chicken broth
 1½ teaspoons finely chopped fresh mint
 1  medium lemon, cut into 6 slices

2 servings

Heat oven to 400°. Pat inside and outside of duck dry
with paper towels. In small bowl, combine 1 tablespoon mint, lemon rind and juice, and 1 tablespoon
butter; mix well. Rub butter mixture inside cavity.
Place duck in 9-inch-square baking pan. In small
saucepan, combine remaining 2 tablespoons butter,
the pepper, and salt. Heat over low heat until butter
melts. Brush over outside of duck.

Roast duck until skin is brown and crisp and duck is
desired doneness, 40 to 60 minutes, basting frequently with pan juices. Transfer duck to heated
serving platter. Set aside and keep warm. Pour pan
juices into medium saucepan. Add stock. Cook
over medium heat until reduced by one-half.
Remove from heat. Add 1½ teaspoons mint and
lemon slices. Let stand about 2 minutes. Arrange
lemon slices on duck; pour sauce over lemon slices
and duck.

## Grilled Teal

 4  whole teal, skin on
 1  whole lemon, quartered
      Olive oil
      Salt and pepper
 8  whole juniper berries
 4  celery tops with leaves
 4  small potatoes
 4  small white onions
      Dried oregano leaves, optional

4 servings

Start charcoal briquets in grill. Pat cavities and out-
sides of ducks dry with paper towels. Rub each duck
cavity with one lemon quarter, then with olive oil.
Set aside lemon quarters. Sprinkle cavity with salt
and pepper. Inside each cavity, place 2 juniper berries, 1 celery top, 1 potato, and 1 onion. Tie drumsticks across cavity with wet kitchen string. Tuck
wing tips behind back. Rub outside of each duck
with lemon quarter, then with olive oil. Sprinkle
with salt, pepper, and oregano.

When charcoal briquets are covered with ash,
spread them evenly in grill. Place grate above hot
coals. Grill ducks until desired doneness, 15 to 35
minutes, turning once or twice and brushing with
olive oil.

TIP: This recipe also works well on a rotisserie.
Skewer ducks as described in photo sequence on
page 108.

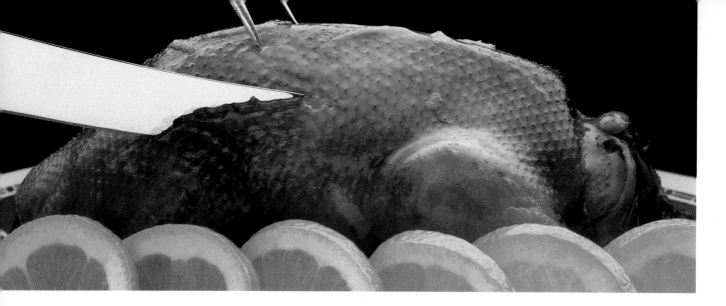

## Duck with Orange Sauce ↑

½ cup chopped onion
½ cup chopped apple
¼ cup chopped celery
2 whole canvasbacks or other large wild ducks, or 3 or 4 smaller wild ducks, skin on

ORANGE SAUCE:
2 tablespoons butter or margarine
2 tablespoons all-purpose flour
2 teaspoons sugar
2 teaspoons grated orange peel
¾ teaspoon salt
⅛ teaspoon dry mustard
⅔ cup fresh orange juice
⅓ cup duck stock (page 145) or chicken broth
¼ cup orange marmalade
2 tablespoons orange liqueur, optional
Orange slices for garnish, optional

4 servings

Heat oven to 350°. In small mixing bowl, combine onion, apple, and celery; mix well. Divide mixture; stuff into duck cavities. Place ducks on rack in roasting pan. Bake for 45 minutes.

While ducks are baking, prepare orange sauce. In small saucepan, melt butter over medium heat. Remove from heat. Blend in flour. Stir in sugar, orange peel, salt, and dry mustard. Blend in orange juice and stock. Cook over medium heat, stirring constantly, until thickened and bubbly. Add marmalade; cook and stir until marmalade melts. Remove from heat. Blend in orange liqueur. Cover and keep warm.

When ducks have baked for 45 minutes, brush lightly with orange sauce. Continue baking until ducks are tender, about 45 minutes longer, brushing with sauce once or twice. Discard vegetable stuffing. Garnish ducks with orange slices. Serve with extra sauce.

## Wine-Braised Duck

¼ cup all-purpose flour
¼ teaspoon salt
¼ teaspoon pepper
2 mallards or other large wild ducks, cut up
2 tablespoons butter or margarine
2 tablespoons vegetable oil
1 medium onion, chopped
2 medium shallots, minced
1 cup red wine
1 cup duck stock (page 145) or chicken broth
8 ounces fresh mushrooms, sliced
1 small bay leaf
1 teaspoon dried thyme leaves
1 teaspoon dried rosemary leaves
1 tablespoon snipped fresh parsley
3 tablespoons cold water
2 tablespoons all-purpose flour
Salt and pepper

4 or 5 servings

On a sheet of waxed paper, mix ¼ cup flour, the salt, and pepper. Dip duck pieces in flour, turning to coat. In Dutch oven, melt butter in oil over medium heat. Add duck pieces; brown on all sides. Remove duck pieces with slotted spoon; set aside.

Add onion and shallots to Dutch oven. Cook and stir over medium heat until tender. Return duck pieces to Dutch oven. Add wine, stock, mushrooms, bay leaf, thyme, rosemary, and parsley. Heat to boiling. Reduce heat; cover. Simmer until duck pieces are tender, 1 to 1¾ hours. With slotted spoon, transfer duck pieces to heated serving platter. Set aside and keep warm. Remove and discard bay leaf. Skim excess fat from cooking liquid. In small bowl, blend water and 2 tablespoons flour. Blend into cooking liquid. Cook over medium heat, stirring constantly, until thickened and bubbly. Season with salt and pepper to taste. Serve sauce over duck pieces.

## Louisiana Boiled Duck

3 quarts water
1 package (3 ounces) crab and shrimp boil mix*
2 or 3 whole ring-necked ducks or other medium
   wild ducks, skin on
   Garlic salt
   Pepper
4 or 6 slices bacon, optional

3 to 5 servings

In large Dutch oven or stock pot, heat water to boiling. Add crab and shrimp boil mix. Return to boiling. Boil 5 minutes. Add ducks. Return to boiling. Reduce heat; cover. Simmer until ducks are tender, about 1½ hours.

Heat oven to 350°. Remove ducks from liquid. Drain and pat dry with paper towels. Place ducks, breast-side up, in roasting pan. Sprinkle with garlic salt and pepper. Place two slices bacon across each duck. Bake until ducks and bacon are browned, 15 to 20 minutes.

*TIP: Crab and shrimp boil mix is available in seafood markets, or in the seafood section of large supermarkets.

## Duck Breasts with Bacon and Onions

*Many people comment that wild ducks, especially diving ducks, taste like liver. This recipe takes advantage of that resemblance.*

 4 boneless breast halves from 2 wild ducks
½ to 1 cup brandy
¼ cup all-purpose flour
¼ teaspoon salt
⅛ teaspoon pepper
 8 slices bacon, cut up
 1 medium onion, very coarsely chopped

4 servings

In medium mixing bowl, combine duck breast halves and enough brandy to cover meat. Cover bowl with plastic wrap. Marinate in refrigerator 1 to 2 hours. Drain breast halves; discard brandy. Pat breast halves dry with paper towels. On a sheet of waxed paper, mix flour, salt, and pepper. Dip breast halves in flour, turning to coat. Set aside breast halves. Discard excess flour mixture.

In large skillet, fry bacon over medium heat until crisp. Remove bacon with fork; set aside. Add floured duck breast halves. Fry over medium heat until browned on one side. Turn breast halves over. Add onion. Continue cooking, rearranging breast halves and onions once or twice, until breast halves are desired doneness and onions are tender-crisp. Serve with bacon.

## Duck-Breast Rumaki ↑

*Duck breast takes the place of chicken livers in this traditional appetizer.*

 2 boneless breast halves from 1 wild duck
½ cup sake or dry sherry
 1 tablespoon soy sauce
 1 tablespoon peanut oil
 1 teaspoon minced fresh gingerroot, optional
 8 to 10 slices bacon, cut in half
16 to 20 canned whole water chestnuts

16 to 20 appetizers

Cut each breast half into 8 to 10 pieces, about 1 inch across each. In small mixing bowl, blend sake, soy sauce, oil, and gingerroot. Add duck pieces; stir to coat. Marinate at room temperature for up to 1 hour. Place one duck chunk and one water chestnut on a piece of bacon. Wrap bacon around duck and water chestnut. Secure with toothpick. Repeat with remaining ingredients. Heat oven to broil and/or 550°. Arrange appetizers on broiler pan. Broil 3 to 4 inches from broiler until bacon is just crisp, about 10 minutes, turning once.

## Duck in Corn Bread Stuffing

Follow recipe on page 112 for Doves in Corn Bread Stuffing, except substitute 2 wild duck breasts, skinned, boned, and cut into ¾-inch strips, for doves. Proceed as directed. Bake for 1 hour.

## Spicy Duck Stir-Fry with Peanuts ↑

*1 large wild duck breast or 2 smaller wild duck breasts, skinned and boned.*

MARINADE:
- 1 tablespoon soy sauce
- 1 tablespoon vegetable oil
- 1 tablespoon cornstarch

SAUCE:
- ¼ cup chicken broth or water
- 2 tablespoons soy sauce
- 1 tablespoon sherry
- 2 teaspoons red wine vinegar
- 1 teaspoon cornstarch
- 1 teaspoon sugar
- ½ teaspoon sesame oil

- 2 tablespoons vegetable oil
- 2 tablespoons minced fresh gingerroot
- ¼ to ½ teaspoon crushed red pepper flakes
- ½ cup salted peanuts
- ¼ cup sliced green onions
  Hot cooked rice

2 or 3 servings

Cut duck breast into ¾-inch pieces. In small mixing bowl, blend all marinade ingredients. Add duck pieces. Stir to coat. Refrigerate 30 to 60 minutes.

In small mixing bowl, blend all sauce ingredients. Set aside. In wok or medium skillet, heat 2 tablespoons oil over medium-high heat. Add gingerroot and pepper flakes. Stir-fry about 30 seconds. Add duck mixture. Stir-fry just until duck is firm. Add peanuts. Stir-fry until golden, about 45 seconds. Add sauce and green onions. Stir-fry until thickened and translucent. Serve with hot cooked rice.

## Mississippi Duck Gumbo

BROTH:
- 4 or 5 widgeon or other medium wild ducks, skinned or skin on
- 1 medium onion, cut up
- 2 carrots, cut into 2-inch pieces
- ⅓ cup snipped fresh parsley, optional
- 1 bay leaf
- 1 to 2 quarts water

ROUX:
- ¾ cup vegetable oil
- ¾ cup all-purpose flour

- 6 medium onions, finely chopped
- 3 medium green peppers, finely chopped
- 2 cups finely chopped celery
- 3 cloves garlic, minced
- 1 can (28 ounces) whole tomatoes, drained and cut up
- 1 to 2 tablespoons Worcestershire sauce
- 1 tablespoon plus 1½ teaspoons salt
- 1½ to 2 teaspoons pepper
- ½ teaspoon dried oregano leaves
- ½ teaspoon dried thyme leaves
- 1 package (10 ounces) frozen okra cuts
  Hot cooked rice

About 4 quarts

In large stockpot, combine all broth ingredients, adding enough water to cover ducks. Heat to boiling. Reduce heat; cover. Simmer until ducks are tender, 1 to 1½ hours. Remove ducks. Strain and reserve broth; discard vegetables. Remove duck meat from bones. Cut meat into bite-sized pieces; set aside. Discard skin and bones. Skim broth; strain through several layers of cheesecloth. Measure 1 quart broth; set aside. Reserve any remaining broth for use in other recipes.

In large stockpot, heat oil over medium heat. Blend in flour. Cook, stirring constantly, until deep golden brown, about 30 minutes. Carefully stir in onions, green pepper, celery, and garlic. Cook, stirring constantly, until vegetables are tender. Stir in duck meat, reserved broth, and remaining ingredients except okra and rice. Heat just to boiling, stirring occasionally. Reduce heat. Simmer, uncovered, for about 30 minutes, stirring occasionally. Add okra. Stir to break apart. Simmer 30 minutes. Serve over hot cooked rice.

*Variation:* For easier gumbo, cook ducks in pressure cooker as directed on page 129, or use 4 cups leftover cooked duck, goose, or turkey. Use 1 quart duck stock (page 145) or ready-to-serve chicken broth. Prepare flour-oil roux as described above. Continue as directed.

# Duck and Pistachio Terrine

*This elegant country-style terrine is wonderful on a buffet table, and equally at home carried in a picnic basket with a loaf of crusty French bread and a bottle of burgundy.*

1 clove garlic, minced
1 teaspoon dried thyme leaves
1 teaspoon dried rosemary leaves, crushed
1 teaspoon salt
¼ teaspoon pepper
¾ cup dry sherry
2 boneless breast halves from 1 mallard, cut into 2-inch chunks
¾ pound boneless fatty pork roast or chops, cut into 2-inch cubes
¼ cup brandy
½ cup red wine
4 boneless breast halves from 2 teal or other small wild ducks
8 slices bacon
¼ cup coarsely chopped pistachios

1 terrine

In medium mixing bowl, blend garlic, thyme, rosemary, salt, pepper, and sherry. Add mallard pieces and cubed pork; stir to coat. Cover bowl with plastic wrap; set aside. In small mixing bowl, combine brandy and wine. Add teal breasts. Cover bowl with plastic wrap. Refrigerate both bowls for at least 8 hours or overnight.

Heat oven to 325°. Line a loaf pan with bacon slices by placing four slices crosswise on the bottom and up the sides, allowing the excess bacon to hang over the edge of the pan. Cut two bacon slices in half. Place two halves up each end of the pan. Set aside remaining two slices.

Drain marinade from mallard mixture, reserving ¼ cup marinade. In food processor, chop mallard mixture to medium consistency. Mix in reserved marinade. Pack half the chopped meat into prepared pan. Arrange teal breast halves on chopped meat. Sprinkle pistachios over breast halves. Pack remaining chopped meat into pan. Fold bacon ends over top of meat. Place two remaining bacon slices on top of loaf. Cover with aluminum foil, pressing onto bacon pieces. Seal well around edges.

Place filled loaf pan into 12 × 8-inch baking dish. Place on oven shelf. Add boiling water to baking dish, 1 to 1½ inches deep. Bake for 1½ hours. Remove loaf pan from baking dish. Allow to cool, covered, for 1 hour. Place a foil-wrapped brick on top of foil-covered loaf pan. Refrigerate, weighted, at least overnight. To serve, remove foil. Loosen edges. Invert onto plate. Scrape away any loose fat and gelatinous juices.

## Goose in Gravy ↑

2 cups leftover goose gravy or beef gravy
½ cup dry white wine or sherry
1 tablespoon Worcestershire sauce
1 cup sliced fresh mushrooms
1 small onion, finely chopped
2 tablespoons butter or margarine
4 cups sliced cooked goose
2 tablespoons sliced ripe olives
1½ teaspoons lemon juice
Salt and pepper
Hot cooked wild rice or buttered toast points

4 to 6 servings

In medium saucepan, heat gravy over medium heat until bubbly, stirring occasionally. Stir in wine and Worcestershire sauce; set aside. In medium skillet, cook and stir mushrooms and onion in butter over medium heat until onion is tender. Add to gravy mixture. Stir in goose, olives and lemon juice; add salt and pepper to taste. Cook over medium-low heat, stirring occasionally, until meat is heated through, about 5 minutes. Serve over hot cooked rice.

## Sesame Duck Cabbage Salad

2 teaspoons butter or margarine
2 tablespoons sliced almonds
2 tablespoons sesame seed
3 cups shredded red cabbage
3 cups shredded green cabbage
1 to 2 cups shredded cooked duck
2 green onions, sliced
1 package (3 ounces) chicken-flavor oriental dry noodle soup mix

DRESSING:
3 tablespoons red wine vinegar
3 tablespoons vegetable oil
2 tablespoons sugar
1 teaspoon sesame oil
¼ teaspoon salt
¼ teaspoon pepper

6 to 8 servings

In small skillet, melt butter over medium-low heat. Add almonds and sesame seed. Cook until light golden brown, stirring constantly. Remove from heat; cool.

In large bowl, combine almond mixture, red and green cabbage, duck, and onions. Sprinkle dry soup seasoning over salad. Break dry noodles into small pieces; add to salad. Mix well. In small bowl, blend all dressing ingredients. Pour over salad, tossing gently to coat. Serve immediately.

## Mandarin Duck Salad ● VERY FAST ↑

*This salad, made with leftover cooked duck, is a lovely blend of tastes, textures, and colors.*

2 teaspoons butter or margarine
½ cup sliced almonds

DRESSING:
½ cup olive oil
¼ cup rice wine vinegar or red wine vinegar
1 tablespoon grated onion
¼ teaspoon salt
¼ teaspoon pepper

SALAD:
12 ounces fresh spinach, washed, trimmed, and
    torn into bite-sized pieces
1 cup shredded cooked duck
1 cup sliced fresh mushrooms
1 small red onion, thinly sliced
1 can (11 ounces) Mandarin orange segments,
    drained

4 to 6 servings

In small skillet, melt butter over medium-low heat. Add almonds. Cook until light golden brown, stirring constantly. Remove from heat; cool.

In small bowl, blend all dressing ingredients. Set aside. In medium bowl, combine all salad ingredients and toasted almonds. Just before serving, add dressing to salad; toss gently to coat.

## Goose and Wild Rice Casserole

2 cups water
½ cup uncooked wild rice, rinsed
½ teaspoon salt
¼ cup butter or margarine
8 ounces fresh mushrooms, sliced
3 tablespoons all-purpose flour
2 teaspoons instant chicken bouillon granules
½ teaspoon salt
1 can (12 ounces) evaporated milk
⅓ cup water
1½ to 2 cups cut-up cooked goose
1 can (8 ounces) sliced water chestnuts, drained
1 jar (2 ounces) sliced pimiento, drained
½ cup sliced almonds

4 to 6 servings

In medium saucepan, combine 2 cups water, the rice, and ½ teaspoon salt. Heat to boiling, stirring once. Reduce heat; cover. Simmer until rice is just tender, 30 to 45 minutes. Drain; set aside.

Heat oven to 350°. Grease 1½-quart casserole; set aside. In medium skillet, melt butter over medium heat. Add mushrooms. Cook and stir until just tender. Stir in flour, bouillon granules, and ½ teaspoon salt. Blend in milk and ⅓ cup water. Cook, stirring constantly, until thickened and bubbly, about 5 minutes. Remove from heat. Stir in goose, water chestnuts, and pimiento. Pour into prepared casserole. Sprinkle with almonds. Cover. Bake 30 minutes. Remove cover. Bake until casserole is hot and bubbly, 15 to 30 minutes longer.

# Stuffing Recipes

Upland game birds and waterfowl should be stuffed just before roasting. Pack the stuffing in lightly, allowing room for expansion.

Each of the recipes in this section makes about 5 cups stuffing — enough for a whole goose or turkey, or four pheasants or ducks. Stuffing can also be baked separately as a side dish to accompany roasts, grilled meats, or other main courses. Place it in a greased 1½-quart casserole. Bake, covered, at 350° for 30 minutes. Uncover, and continue baking until the stuffing is hot, 15 to 25 minutes. If you are baking stuffing as a side dish to accompany a roast, spoon pan juices from the roast over the stuffing several times to add flavor.

## ← Corn Bread Stuffing ◈ LOW-FAT

      5  slices bacon
      3  tablespoons butter or margarine
      1  small onion, chopped
    ⅓  cup chopped celery
    1½  cups sliced fresh mushrooms
      4  cups corn bread stuffing mix
    ⅓  cup snipped fresh parsley
      1  cup game bird stock (page 145) or
         chicken broth
      1  egg, beaten

In medium skillet, fry bacon over medium-low heat until crisp. Remove bacon to paper towels to drain. Crumble bacon; set aside. Over medium heat, melt butter in bacon drippings. Add onion and celery. Cook and stir for 3 minutes. Add mushrooms. Cook and stir until vegetables are just tender, about 2 minutes longer. Remove from heat. In medium mixing bowl, combine corn bread stuffing mix, parsley, reserved crumbled bacon, and vegetable mixture. Mix well. Add broth and egg. Mix well.

## Apricot Stuffing ◈ LOW-FAT

*Good as a stuffing for any game bird, this also makes an excellent side dish to serve with small game or venison.*

      7  or 8 slices whole wheat or white bread (or
         half whole wheat, half white bread)
    ½  cup cut-up dried apricots
    ½  cup chopped pecans or walnuts
      1  teaspoon dried crushed sage leaves
      1  teaspoon dried parsley flakes
    ½  teaspoon salt
    ¼  teaspoon pepper
      1  medium onion, chopped
      1  cup chopped celery
    ¼  cup butter or margarine
      1  cup game bird stock (page 145) or
         chicken broth

Heat oven to 325° Place bread directly on oven rack. Bake until bread is dry, 5 to 10 minutes. Cool. Cut into ½-inch cubes; there should be about 5 cups bread cubes. Place bread cubes in medium mixing bowl. Add apricots, pecans, sage, parsley, salt, and pepper. Mix well; set aside.

In medium skillet, cook and stir onion and celery in butter over medium heat until tender. Stir into bread-cube mixture. Add stock; mix well.

NOTE: For moister stuffing, or if stuffing is to be cooked separately, add 1 beaten egg with stock.

## Spicy Sausage Dressing

*Use this as a stuffing for waterfowl, or bake as a side dish with a venison roast.*

- ¼ cup butter or margarine
- 5 cups cubed French bread, ¾-inch cubes
- ½ pound spicy pork sausage
- 1 small onion, chopped
- ⅓ cup thinly sliced celery
- 1 medium apple, cored and chopped
- ½ cup chopped pecans or walnuts
- ⅓ cup game bird stock (page 145) or chicken broth

In large skillet, melt butter over medium-low heat. Add bread cubes, stirring to coat. Cook and stir over medium heat until bread cubes are lightly toasted. Transfer bread cubes to large mixing bowl; set aside.

In same skillet, cook sausage over medium heat until meat loses pink color, stirring to break up pieces. Add onion and celery. Cook and stir until vegetables are tender and pork sausage is cooked through. Add sausage mixture to bread cubes. Add apple and pecans; mix well. Add stock; mix well.

NOTE: For moister stuffing, or if stuffing is to be cooked separately, add 1 beaten egg with stock.

## Onion-Bread Dressing ◆ LOW-FAT

*This is a very traditional dressing.*

- 1 medium onion, cut in half lengthwise and thinly sliced
- ¼ cup butter or margarine
- 4½ cups herb-seasoned croutons
- 2 teaspoons dried parsley flakes
- ½ teaspoon salt
- ½ teaspoon dried crushed sage leaves, optional
- ½ teaspoon dried basil leaves
- ¼ teaspoon dried marjoram leaves
- 1 cup game bird stock (page 145) or chicken broth
- 1 egg

In medium skillet, cook and stir onion in butter over medium heat until tender. Remove from heat; set aside. In medium mixing bowl, combine croutons, parsley, salt, sage, basil, and marjoram; mix well. Stir in onions and butter. In small mixing bowl, blend stock and egg. Add to crouton mixture; mix well.

## Gingered Rice Stuffing ◆ LOW-FAT ↑

*A mixture of white, brown, and wild rice makes this stuffing very attractive. Use as a stuffing for any game bird, or as an interesting side dish.*

- 2 cups chopped celery
- 1 medium onion, chopped
- 2 teaspoons grated fresh gingerroot
- ½ cup butter or margarine
- 2 cups cooked rice
- 1 can (8 ounces) sliced water chestnuts, drained
- ⅓ cup unseasoned dry bread crumbs

In medium skillet, cook and stir celery, onion, and gingerroot in butter over medium heat until tender. In medium mixing bowl, combine vegetable mixture and remaining ingredients; mix well.

# Game Stock

Good stock is fundamental to good cooking. It's used as the base for sauces, and as the cooking liquid in many recipes. Game stock is made by boiling the bones of big-game animals, birds, or small game, usually with vegetables and seasonings. It adds more flavor to recipes than commercial chicken or beef broth. For convenience, freeze stock in 1-cup batches (page 49). Or, can it in the pressure cooker (page 153). Leave ½ inch head space in pint jars; process at 10 pounds pressure for 20 minutes.

If you make a large batch of stock, you may want to try a technique used by professional chefs. Prepare the stock without adding salt, then strain it through a double thickness of cheesecloth. Allow the strained stock to cool completely, then skim off any fat. Boil the strained, skimmed stock until it is reduced by half to make a *demi-glace* (half glaze), which is the base for many classic French sauces. Reducing the *demi-glace* even further produces a hard, rubbery glaze that can be cut into small chunks and frozen. A small chunk of the glaze added to a sauce or braising liquid intensifies the flavor of the dish without adding liquid. If a recipe calls for a teaspoon of instant bouillon granules, you can substitute a small chunk of glaze and a bit of salt.

## Venison Stock →

*Browning the bones in the oven makes the stock rich and dark. Venison stock requires long cooking to bring out all the flavor from the large bones.*

 Enough deer, antelope, elk, or moose bones
  to fit stockpot (5 to 10 pounds)
 4 to 6 carrots, cut into 2-inch pieces
 3 or 4 stalks celery, cut into 2-inch pieces
 2 medium onions, cut into quarters
 2 bay leaves
 10 whole black peppercorns
 4 or 5 sprigs fresh parsley
 1 sprig fresh thyme, or ½ teaspoon dried
  thyme leaves

About 3 quarts

### How to Prepare Venison Stock

ARRANGE bones in roasting pan. Heat oven to 450°. Roast until well browned, about 1 hour, turning bones once during roasting. Transfer bones to stock pot.

LOOSEN browned bits from roaster by stirring, adding 1 cup water if necessary. Pour liquid into large measuring cup. Skim fat; discard. Add liquid to stockpot.

ADD remaining ingredients to stockpot. Cover bones with cold water. Heat to boiling over medium-high heat. Reduce heat. Skim foam from top of stock. Simmer for about 8 hours, skimming periodically, and adding additional water as necessary to keep bones covered.

STRAIN stock through a double thickness of cheese-cloth. Discard bones and vegetables. Pour stock back into stockpot. Heat to boiling over medium-high heat. Cook until reduced to about 3 quarts. Cool slightly. Refrigerate overnight. Skim any solidified fat from top.

## Game Bird Stock →
(Pheasant, Partridge, Grouse, Turkey, or Waterfowl)

*Save the backbone and neck when portioning birds, and any bones left after boning, until you have enough to make stock. Game bird stock cooks quicker than venison stock.*

1½ to 2 pounds uncooked game bird backs
     and bones
  1 small onion, quartered
  1 stalk celery, cut into 1-inch pieces
  1 carrot, cut into 1-inch pieces
 ¼ cup snipped fresh parsley
 ½ teaspoon dried marjoram leaves
 ½ teaspoon dried thyme leaves
  6 whole black peppercorns
  2 whole cloves
  1 bay leaf
1¼ teaspoons salt, optional
  4 to 6 cups cold water

About 3 cups stock

In large saucepan, combine all ingredients, adding enough water to completely cover the bones and vegetables. Heat to boiling over medium-high heat. Reduce heat. Skim foam from top of stock. Simmer for 1½ to 2 hours, skimming periodically. Strain through a double thickness of cheesecloth. Discard bones and vegetables. Cool stock slightly. Refrigerate overnight. Skim any solidified fat from top.

## Rabbit Stock

Follow recipe above, substituting 1½ to 2 pounds rabbit backs, ribs, and other bones for the game bird bones. Continue as directed, cooking 2 to 2½ hours.

# Sauces & Marinades

Sauces enhance the flavor of simply prepared game. Game stock is ideal for use in the sauce recipes on these pages that call for stock. If you substitute prepared chicken or beef broth for the game stock, you may wish to reduce the amount of salt in the recipe.

Marinades tenderize tougher cuts of game and add flavor. Most marinades are combinations of oil and an acidic ingredient such as lemon juice, wine, or vinegar, with herbs and spices added for flavor. Experiment with different seasoning combinations to create your own "house blend."

## Cherry Sauce  ↑

*Dark cherries seem a natural complement to waterfowl. This sauce is also good with roast big game.*

1 can (16 ounces) pitted dark sweet cherries, drained, juice reserved
   Cherry-flavored brandy, plain brandy, or water
2 tablespoons cornstarch
2 tablespoons lemon juice
   Dash salt
2 tablespoons honey
2 tablespoons butter or margarine, cut up

About 2½ cups

In 2-cup measure, combine reserved cherry juice and enough brandy to equal 1⅔ cups. In medium saucepan, blend cherry juice mixture, cornstarch, lemon juice, and salt. Cook over medium heat, stirring constantly, until translucent and bubbly, 5 to 7 minutes. Stir in honey. Add butter. Cook and stir over low heat until butter melts. Stir in cherries. Cook and stir until hot. Serve sauce warm.

## Italian Green Sauce

*This sauce is often served in Italy with grilled meats. It's good with any type of game.*

¼ cup soft bread crumbs
2 teaspoons white vinegar
1 hard-cooked egg yolk, chopped
1 or 2 anchovy fillets, cut up, optional
2 teaspoons capers
¾ cup snipped fresh parsley
2 teaspoons finely chopped onion
1 clove garlic, minced
⅓ to ½ cup olive oil

About ¾ cup

In small mixing bowl, combine bread crumbs and vinegar; mix well. Let stand 10 minutes. In another small bowl, combine egg yolk, anchovy fillets, and capers. Mash with a fork. Add yolk mixture, parsley, onion, and garlic to bread crumb mixture; mix well. Blend in oil until sauce is desired consistency. Let stand at room temperature for at least 30 minutes before serving. Stir before serving. Serve sauce at room temperature.

NOTE: For a smoother consistency, combine all ingredients in blender or food processor. Process just until smooth. Sauce prepared in blender may be served immediately.

## Dried Mushroom Sauce

*Dried morel mushrooms enliven this variation of Easy Velouté Sauce (right). The mushroom-soaking liquid is used to replace the game stock.*

½ ounce dried morels or other mushrooms
    (about ⅔ cup)
1 cup warm water
2 tablespoons butter or margarine
2 tablespoons all-purpose flour
¼ teaspoon salt
    Dash white pepper
    Dash ground nutmeg
¼ cup whipping cream or half-and-half

About 1½ cups

Break dried mushrooms into pieces. In small mixing bowl, combine mushrooms and water; stir. Let rehydrate 15 minutes. Remove mushrooms with slotted spoon; set aside. Reserve ¾ cup soaking liquid.

In small saucepan, melt butter over medium-low heat. Stir in flour, salt, pepper, and nutmeg. Blend in cream, and reserved mushrooms and liquid. Cook over medium heat until thickened and bubbly, 5 to 7 minutes. Serve sauce warm.

## Madeira Game Sauce

*Excellent with any big-game roast or steaks.*

3 tablespoons butter or margarine
3 tablespoons all-purpose flour
1 cup venison stock (page 144) or beef broth
2 tablespoons currant jelly
2 tablespoons Madeira wine

About 1 cup

In small saucepan, melt butter over medium-low heat. Stir in flour. Blend in stock. Cook over medium heat until thickened and bubbly, 5 to 7 minutes. Add jelly; stir until melted. Add Madeira; heat just to boiling. Serve sauce warm.

## Easy Velouté Sauce

*Serve this sauce with birds or small game. Create your own sauce variations by adding fresh herbs.*

2 tablespoons butter or margarine
2 tablespoons all-purpose flour
¼ teaspoon salt
    Dash white pepper
¾ cup game bird stock (page 145) or
    chicken broth
¼ cup whipping cream or half-and-half

About 1 cup

In small saucepan, melt butter over medium-low heat. Stir in flour, salt, and pepper. Blend in stock and cream. Cook over medium heat, stirring constantly, until thickened and bubbly, 5 to 7 minutes. Serve sauce warm.

## Big-Game Brown Sauce  LOW-FAT VERY FAST ↑

*In classic French cooking, many sauces are based on brown sauce, made by reducing rich stock. The following recipes are variations on that idea, simplified for the home cook.*

- ⅓ cup finely chopped onion
- 1 small carrot, finely chopped
- 3 tablespoons butter or margarine
- ¼ cup dry white wine
- 2 tablespoons all-purpose flour
- 1 cup venison stock (page 144) or beef broth
- 1 teaspoon lemon juice or vinegar
  Salt and freshly ground black pepper

About 1 cup

In medium skillet, cook and stir onion and carrot in butter over medium heat until tender. Stir in wine. Cook, stirring occasionally, until reduced by half. Stir in flour. Blend in stock and lemon juice. Cook over medium-high heat, stirring constantly, until thickened and bubbly, 5 to 7 minutes. Strain sauce if desired. Add salt and pepper to taste. Serve warm.

*Richer Big-Game Brown Sauce:* Cook onion and carrot in butter as directed in recipe for Big-Game Brown Sauce. Blend in wine; reduce as directed. Stir in flour. Blend in ¾ cup reduced venison stock (*demi-glace,* page 144), ¼ cup white wine, and lemon juice. Cook over medium-high heat, stirring constantly, until thickened and bubbly, 5 to 7 minutes. Strain sauce if desired. Add salt and pepper to taste. Serve warm.

*Quick and Easy Big-Game Brown Sauce:* Cook onion and carrot in butter as directed in recipe for Big-Game Brown Sauce. Blend in wine; reduce as directed. Omit flour. In small bowl, blend 1 package (.87 ounces) brown gravy mix and 1 cup water. Blend gravy mixture and lemon juice into onion mixture. Cook over medium-high heat, stirring constantly, until thickened and bubbly, 5 to 7 minutes. Strain sauce if desired. If necessary, add salt and pepper to taste. Serve warm.

## Pepper-Flavored Brown Sauce  LOW-FAT VERY FAST

In small saucepan, combine 1 cup venison stock, 6 to 10 whole black peppercorns, ¼ to ½ teaspoon dry mustard, and a dash cayenne pepper. Heat to boiling. Reduce heat; cover. Simmer 10 minutes. Strain stock and discard peppercorns. Follow recipe for Big-Game Brown Sauce, using pepper-flavored stock, and substituting vermouth for white wine. Continue as directed.

## Orange-Flavored Brown Sauce  LOW-FAT VERY FAST

In small bowl, combine 3 tablespoons grated orange peel and 2 cups boiling water. Let stand 5 minutes. Drain; set peel aside. Follow recipe for Big-Game Brown Sauce, omitting carrot, and substituting ¼ cup dry red wine and ¼ cup orange juice for the white wine. Continue as directed. When sauce is thickened and bubbly, stir in reserved orange peel, 2 tablespoons cognac (optional), and 1 tablespoon red currant jelly. Cook over medium heat until jelly melts, stirring constantly.

## Lemon-Garlic Marinade

*This marinade is especially good with upland game birds.*

- ½ cup fresh lemon juice
- ½ cup olive oil or vegetable oil
- 2 teaspoons dried oregano leaves
- 1 teaspoon prepared Dijon-style mustard
- 3 cloves garlic, minced
- ⅛ teaspoon freshly ground black pepper

In small saucepan, combine all ingredients. Heat until bubbly. Cool to room temperature. Marinate game birds or meat at least 3 hours, or overnight, turning occasionally, before grilling or broiling.

## Greek-Style Marinade

*Try marinating big-game steaks in this blend before grilling. This is also excellent with ducks.*

- ½ cup olive oil or vegetable oil
- ½ cup sweet vermouth
- 1 tablespoon lemon juice
- ¾ teaspoon dried tarragon leaves
- 1 small red onion, thinly sliced and separated into rings
- ⅛ teaspoon cracked black pepper

In small saucepan, combine all ingredients. Heat until bubbly. Cool to room temperature. Marinate game birds or meat at least 3 hours, or overnight, turning occasionally, before grilling or broiling.

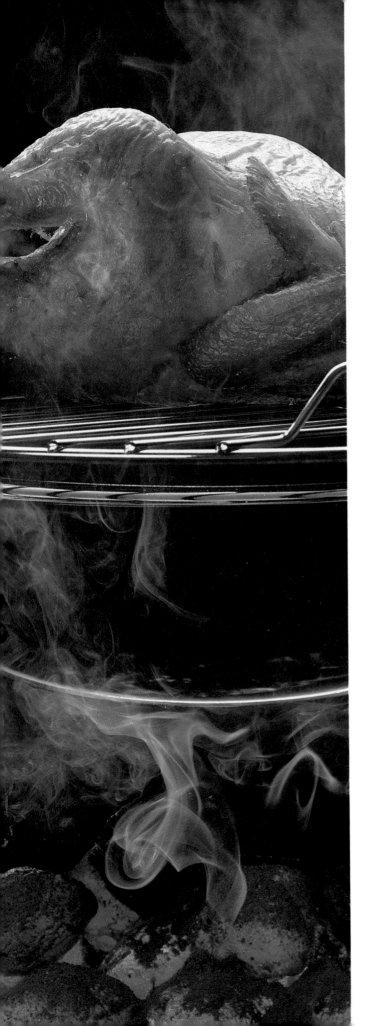

# Smoking Wild Game

Smoke and wild game seem to go together naturally. The tangy, sweet smoke flavor is reminiscent of a day in the woods or field.

There are two basic methods of smoking. In *hot smoking,* or smoke cooking, temperatures are higher than 120° (generally 150° to 300°); in *cold smoking,* below 120°. Hot smoking is not a preservation technique, but simply a cooking method. Old-time smokehouses used cold smoking to preserve heavily brined meat. But preserving with cold smoke is tricky, in some cases requiring several weeks. In this book, cold smoking is used as a flavoring technique only.

All smokers work on the same principle. The meat is hung or laid on racks in an enclosure. A heat source, usually at the bottom of the enclosure, burns wood to provide smoke. Vent holes allow some smoke to escape so it doesn't become stale, and also help regulate the temperature.

A wide variety of smokers is available at sporting-goods stores, but many people make their own. Homemade smokers range from an old refrigerator with a hot plate, to more elaborate brick enclosures. Consult a book on smoking for complete instructions on making smokers.

Many smokers can be used for either hot or cold smoking, depending on the weather and the heat source. If your smoker doesn't have a built-in thermometer, it's helpful to add one (page 150).

Smokers with large electric coils, or those that use charcoal for the heat source, generally are used as hot smokers. Charcoal-fueled units can also serve as cold smokers. Use only a handful of charcoal, rather than a full batch. Monitor the temperature carefully.

Hot smokers often have a pan above the heat source for holding liquid. The heat evaporates the liquid, so the meat is bathed in moist smoke. Game does not dry out as much as in dry heat. Many cooks use beer, broth, and other liquids to add flavor.

Smokers with small electric hot plates for the heat source may not be adequate for smoke cooking, especially in cold weather. These smokers, commonly made of aluminum, are often used for cold smoking.

Wild game, unlike fish, is not always brined before smoking. Many people prefer to smoke it plain, or lightly seasoned. But brining before smoking does add a unique flavor, and makes the meat firmer.

To produce smoke, use trimmings from fruit trees or other hardwoods. Apple and alder add a mild, sweet flavor. Cherry and pear provide a stronger taste. Hickory is the strongest, and is traditionally used with hams and bacon. Cobs from dried corn add an interesting flavor, as do unusual woods like mesquite and sassafras. You can often purchase

149

wood chunks or shavings where smokers are sold, or in large supermarkets. Never use wood from evergreens or softwoods; they give meat a resinous taste.

Soak wood chunks in water for at least an hour before using them. They will produce more smoke, and are less likely to burst into flame than dry chunks. Small chips or sawdust used over small electric hot plates are not usually soaked.

Weather can greatly affect smoking time. In hot weather, even models with small hot plates may get too warm for cold smoking. Cold and windy weather lowers the temperature in any smoker. To increase the smoking temperature, place your smoker out of the wind. If your smoker is electric, slip the shipping carton or other large cardboard box over it for insulation. If it's charcoal-fueled, just add extra charcoal. Should the temperature still not rise enough for hot smoking, smoke the meat for several hours at the low temperature, then finish cooking in the oven.

Judge doneness of hot-smoked meat by checking its temperature with a thermometer. When using cold smoke to flavor meat, use the color of the meat as a guide. A golden color on pheasant, for example, indicates a light smoke flavor, while a deep golden-brown indicates strong smoke. You'll soon learn how much smoke you prefer. After cold smoking, roast the meat in the oven to the desired temperature.

Smoking is an art, requiring a willingness to experiment. Home smokers are imprecise, subject to great variations in heat, moisture, and amount of smoke produced. You must learn how the weather affects smoking, how long your smoker takes to smoke, and what methods you prefer for different game. For future reference, keep a notebook listing recipe used, smoking times, weather conditions, and results.

*Tips for Smoking Wild Game*

SMOKE-COOK game of different sizes at the same time by placing large items on bottom rack and small ones on top rack. Game on top is farther from heat, and also easier to remove if it gets done sooner.

USE a covered barbecue grill as a hot smoker. Pile charcoal briquets on one side and light. Toss wet wood chunks onto ash-covered coals. Place a pan of liquid on grate above the coals. Put game on other side of grate. Close cover, and regulate heat with air vents.

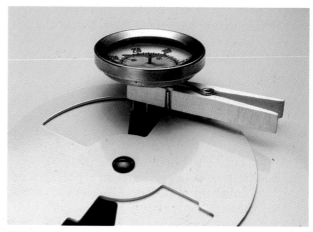

CLIP a deep-frying thermometer into a clothespin and insert the tip into a vent hole if your smoker doesn't have a built-in thermometer. The clothespin keeps the thermometer from coming in contact with hot metal.

## Hot-Smoked Venison Roast ⬦ LOW-FAT →

*Use a boneless deer sirloin tip, rump roast, or rolled top or bottom round. Similarly sized tender antelope, elk, or moose roasts can be substituted.*

> Hickory chunks or other hardwood chunks
> 1½ to 2-pound venison roast, 3 to 4 inches thick
> Bacon fat, butter, or margarine
> Garlic salt or seasoned salt
> 4 to 6 slices bacon
> Beef broth, beer, or water

4 to 6 servings

Start a full load of charcoal briquets in charcoal-fueled hot smoker; plug in electric smoker. Soak 8 to 10 large chunks of hickory (about 1 × 2-inch chunks; use more if chunks are smaller) in a bucket of water for at least 1 hour. Rub roast with bacon fat; sprinkle with garlic salt. Place bacon slices over roast to cover; secure with toothpicks. Insert meat thermometer into thickest part of roast.

When charcoal briquets are covered with ash, or when electric coils are hot, toss wet wood onto hot coals, or place into wood pan of electric smoker. Fill water pan about ⅔ full with broth. Place roast on bottom rack above water pan. Close smoker. Smoke until meat reaches desired temperature (page 54), usually between 2 and 3 hours. If charcoal smoker is not hot enough, open top and bottom vents slightly. Do not open the smoker, except to check meat temperature near the end of cooking. Add additional soaked wood during the last hour of smoking. If a roast of this size is not desired temperature after about 3 hours, remove from smoker; finish roasting in covered pan in 350° oven.

*Variation:* Sear roast on all sides in skillet in hot bacon fat or vegetable oil. Sprinkle with salt; omit bacon slices. Continue as directed.

NOTE: Larger roasts can be hot-smoked, but smoking time will need to be increased. It is the thickness of the roast, not necessarily its weight, that determines hot-smoking time. When smoking time is longer than about 3 hours, it may be necessary to add additional broth to the water pan.

## Hot-Smoked Game Birds or Small Game

Birds and small game may be brined as described on page 152, or smoked without brining. Small birds like quail can brine for 1 or 2 hours. Rabbits and squirrels, and larger birds like pheasant and duck can brine up to 4 hours. Skin-on birds may be brushed with a mixture of 2 tablespoons honey and 2 teaspoons soy sauce, if desired. Small game and skinned birds should be smeared with softened butter or covered with bacon slices. Smoke according to chart at right.

*Hot-smoking Times for Game Birds and Small Game*

| TYPE OF GAME | TYPE OF WOOD | TYPICAL TIME |
|---|---|---|
| Wild Turkey | Apple | 8 to 12 hours (on bottom shelf) |
| Pheasant | Apple | 2 to 3 hours (on bottom shelf) |
| Partridge | Apple, alder | 1 to 2 hours (on bottom shelf) |
| Grouse | Apple | 1 to 2 hours (on bottom shelf) |
| Quail | Apple, alder | 1 to 2 hours (on top shelf) |
| Turkey Breast | Apple | 3 to 4 hours (on top shelf) |
| Large Ducks | Cherry, hickory | 3 to 4 hours (on bottom shelf) |
| Small Ducks | Cherry, hickory | 2 to 3 hours (on bottom shelf) |
| Whole Goose | Pear, cherry | 6 to 12 hours (on bottom shelf) |
| Goose Breast | Pear, cherry | 3 to 4 hours (on bottom shelf) |
| Squirrel | Hickory, alder | 2 to 4 hours (on top shelf) |
| Wild Rabbit | Hickory, mesquite | 3 to 5 hours (on top shelf) |

## Cold-Smoked Game Birds

*Birds smoked in this manner have a firm, dry texture, and are usually served as an appetizer. Rabbits or squirrels can also be smoked with this recipe.*

BRINE:
 2 quarts bottled spring water
 ¾ cup pickling salt
 ½ cup brown sugar
 ¼ cup maple syrup
 3 tablespoons white wine vinegar
 1 tablespoon pickling spice

 2 whole pheasants or wild ducks

*3 or 4 servings*

In medium ceramic or glass mixing bowl, combine all brine ingredients, stirring until salt is dissolved. Add pheasants or ducks. Place a small ceramic plate on top of birds to submerge them completely. Brine birds in refrigerator at least 8 hours or overnight, turning once.

Remove birds from brine; pat dry. Air-dry for ½ hour. Cold-smoke pheasants for 2 to 3 hours, ducks for 3 to 4 hours. Heat oven to 350°. If birds have skin on, roast uncovered until desired doneness, about 1 hour. If birds have been skinned, cover them with cheesecloth which has been saturated with butter, or with slices of bacon. Serve birds hot or cold.

## Cold-Smoked Duck Breasts

Prepare brine as directed above. Add skinned, boned breasts from 3 or 4 ducks. Brine for about 4 hours. Dry as directed above. Cold-smoke for 2 to 3 hours. Rub breasts with softened butter. Bake at 350° until desired doneness, 30 to 45 minutes. Sliced smoked duck breasts make an excellent sandwich to take into the duck blind.

## ← Traditional Venison Jerky ◆ LOW-FAT

SEASONING MIXTURE:
2¼ teaspoons tenderizing salt (e.g. Morton's Tenderquick®)
2¼ teaspoons pickling salt
1½ teaspoons garlic powder
1½ teaspoons pepper

1½ pounds boneless deer, antelope, elk, or moose

*About ¾ pound jerky*

In small bowl or empty spice bottle with shaker top, combine all seasoning-mixture ingredients. Mix well; set aside. Slice venison with the grain into strips about ⅛ inch thick. Arrange in single layer on cutting board. Sprinkle evenly with seasoning mixture, using mixture as though salting heavily. Pound meat lightly with meat mallet. Turn strips over; sprinkle and pound second side.

Arrange meat on smoker racks. Cold-smoke until strips are dry but not brittle, 5 hours or longer, re-arranging racks periodically and adding additional wood chips as necessary. (Hickory, cherry, or mesquite work well in this recipe.) Jerky will become more brittle as it cools. Refrigerate jerky for storage.

## Cold-Smoked Chops with Kraut ◆ LOW-FAT

MARINADE:
 2 or 3 cloves garlic, chopped
 3 tablespoons vegetable oil
 3 tablespoons soy sauce
 1 tablespoon Worcestershire sauce
1½ teaspoons lemon juice

1½ to 2½ pounds big-game chops or steaks, about ¾ inch thick
 2 quarts sauerkraut
 ½ cup apple juice or chicken broth
 ½ cup water

*6 to 8 servings*

In food processor or blender, combine all marinade ingredients; process until smooth. Place chops in a single layer in large glass baking dish. Pour half the marinade over chops. Turn chops over. Cover with remaining marinade. Place plastic wrap directly on surface of chops. Refrigerate 8 hours or overnight.

Drain chops; place on rack of cold smoker. Cold-smoke for 3 to 4 hours. (Pear, cherry, or alder are good woods to use in this recipe.)

Heat oven to 300°. Rinse sauerkraut; drain well. Grease a 13 × 9-inch baking pan. Arrange smoked chops in baking pan. Top with sauerkraut. Pour apple juice and water evenly over sauerkraut. Cover pan with aluminum foil. Bake until meat is desired doneness, 45 minutes to 1 hour.

# Smoky Canned Big-Game Chunks

*Use this meat to make quick stews, or shred and add to barbecue sauce for unusual Sloppy Joes. This is also excellent when used as the cooked game in Big-Game Sandwich Filling, page 78.*

3 or more pounds boneless big-game steaks or other large chunks, ¾ to 1 inch thick

MARINADE (FOR EACH 3 POUNDS MEAT):
½ cup soy sauce
¼ cup vegetable oil
1 teaspoon sugar
1 teaspoon black pepper
3 cloves garlic, chopped
½ teaspoon Worcestershire sauce

CANNING BROTH (FOR EACH 3 POUNDS MEAT):
1 cup venison stock (page 144) or beef broth
¼ cup vinegar
1 teaspoon sugar

1½ pounds meat per pint

Place meat in a single layer in large glass baking dish. In food processor or blender, combine all marinade ingredients; process until smooth. Pour half the marinade over meat. Turn meat over. Cover with remaining marinade. Place plastic wrap directly on surface of meat. Refrigerate at least 3 hours.

Prepare hot smoker as described in Hot-Smoked Venison Roast (page 151). Use 8 to 10 wet chunks of hickory, mesquite, cherry, or alder. Fill water pan about ⅔ full with water. Drain meat; place on top and bottom racks of hot smoker. Top meat with thinly sliced onion if desired. Smoke until meat is medium doneness, usually 2 to 3 hours, basting meat once with marinade and reversing position of racks.

Remove meat from smoker; cool slightly. In medium saucepan, combine all canning-broth ingredients. Heat to boiling. Remove from heat; set aside. Cut meat into 1- to 1½-inch chunks. Follow photo directions below for canning.

## *How to Can Big Game in a Pressure Cooker*

WASH pint jars, bands, and lids in hot, soapy water. Rinse well. Place jars and bands in sink filled with hot, clear water. Place lids in saucepan; cover with hot water. Heat to barely simmering over low heat.

PACK warm smoked chunks into jars, leaving 1 inch space at top. Unsmoked meat cubes can also be canned; cook to rare, and pack while hot. Add boiling broth, leaving 1 inch space at top. Wipe rim with clean cloth.

PLACE warm lid and band on the jar. Tighten firmly but lightly. Place sealed jars on trivet in pressure cooker. Follow pressure-cooker manufacturer's directions for number of jars and amount of water to add to cooker. Heat until 10 pounds pressure is reached, then begin timing. Process for 1¼ hours at 10 pounds pressure.

ALLOW pressure to drop naturally. When pressure has dropped completely, remove jars with tongs. Place in a draft-free place for 12 hours. Check seals according to lid manufacturer's directions. Refrigerate any jars that have not sealed properly; use within 3 days. Store jars in a dark, cool place; use within one year.

# Nutritional Chart

If a recipe has a range of servings, the data below applies to the greater number of servings. If the recipe lists a quantity range for an ingredient, the average was used to calculate the nutritional data. If alternate ingredients are listed, the analysis applies to the first ingredient listed, with one exception: canned broth was used in place of homemade stock. Sauces and optional ingredients are not included in the analysis. Data for pheasants was used in all recipes calling for grouse, partridge, or woodcock. Data for squab was used in recipes calling for dove.

| | Calories | Fat (g) | Sodium (mg) | Protein (mg) | Carbohydrate (mg) | Cholesterol (mg) | Exchanges ❖ |
|---|---|---|---|---|---|---|---|
| Apricot Stuffing (½ c.) | 156 | 9 | 390 | 3 | 17 | 10 | 1 S; ½ Fr; ½ V; 2 F |
| Baked Pheasant in Madeira | 513 | 24 | 540 | 57 | 14 | 175 | 8 LM; 1 C; ½ V |
| Baked Smothered Pheasant | 697 | 40 | 1,310 | 60 | 22 | 215 | 1 S; 8 LM; 1 V; 3 F |
| Barbecued Partridge on Rotisserie (1 bird) | 765 | 33 | 660 | 79 | 32 | 245 | 11½ LM; 2½ C |
| Basque Pheasant | 752 | 44 | 900 | 57 | 33 | 175 | 1 Fr; 8 LM; 1½ C; 4 F |
| Bear Steak Flamade | 373 | 24 | 410 | 25 | 13 | 30 | ½ S; 3 LM; 1½ V; 3 F |
| Bear Stew | 348 | 16 | 530 | 29 | 21 | 0 | 1 S; 3½ LM; 1 V; 1 F |
| Big Game and Onion Casserole Braised in Beer | 248 | 9 | 380 | 27 | 13 | 105 | 3½ VLM; ½ C; 1 V; 1½ F |
| Big Game Baked Round Steak | 292 | 11 | 780 | 34 | 12 | 130 | ½ S; 5 VLM; ½ C; 2 F |
| Big Game Belgium | 753 | 46 | 830 | 56 | 24 | 175 | ½ S; 7½ VLM; 1 C; 1½ V; 8½ F |
| Big Game Goulash | 302 | 16 | 650 | 17 | 24 | 60 | 1½ S; 1½ VLM; 1 V; 3 F |
| Big Game Pie | 554 | 33 | 770 | 20 | 44 | 75 | 3 S; 1½ VLM; 1 V; 6 F |
| Big Game Pot Roast | 422 | 13 | 760 | 51 | 23 | 180 | ½ S; 6½ VLM; 3 V; 2 F |
| Big Game Sandwich Filling (½ c.) | 203 | 9 | 500 | 27 | 2 | 100 | 4 VLM; 1½ F |
| Big Game Swiss Steak | 249 | 9 | 790 | 28 | 13 | 100 | ½ S; 3½ VLM; 1 V; 1½ F |
| Big-Game Brown Sauce (1 Tbsp.) | 29 | 2 | 75 | .3 | 1 | 5 | ½ V; ½ F |
| Big-Game Mincemeat Pie (⅛ recipe) | 707 | 35 | 560 | 12 | 90 | 70 | 1½ S; 1 VLM; 3½ Fr; 1 C; 6½ F |
| Birds in Aspic | 131 | 3.5 | 360 | 22 | .6 | 55 | 3 VLM; ½ F |
| Blue Goose with Cherries | 798 | 48 | 640 | 47 | 44 | 175 | 1½ Fr; 1½ C; 6½ MFM; ½ V; 3 F |
| Brunswick Stew | 336 | 11 | 670 | 31 | 29 | 110 | 1½ S; 3½ VLM; 1½ V; 1½ F |
| Cherry Sauce (¼ c.) | 97 | 2 | 35 | .3 | 12 | 5 | ½ Fr; 1 C; ½ F |
| Chicken-Fried Venison Steaks | 411 | 21 | 630 | 39 | 16 | 200 | 1 S; 5 VLM; ½ M; 3 F |
| Cold-Smoked Chops with Kraut | 241 | 8 | 2,030 | 29 | 13 | 95 | 3½ VLM; 2 V; 1½ F |
| Cold-Smoked Game Birds | 690 | 34 | 1,310 | 83 | 7 | 260 | 12 LM; ½ C |
| Coon Sauce Piquante | | | | | Nutritional information not available | | |
| Coonpfeffer | | | | | Nutritional information not available | | |
| Corn Bread Stuffing (½ c.) | 204 | 7 | 590 | 6 | 29 | 35 | 2 S; ½ V; 1½ F |
| Corned Venison | 233 | 4.5 | 1,630 | 43 | 2 | 160 | 6 VLM; ½ F |
| Corned Venison with Vegetables | 286 | 4 | 1,260 | 35 | 27 | 120 | 1 S; 4 VLM; 2½ V; ½ F |
| Cranberry Braised Raccoon | | | | | Nutritional information not available | | |
| Creamed Turkey Patties | 330 | 24 | 430 | 18 | 7 | 125 | ½ S; 2½ VLM; ½ C; ½ V; 4½ F |
| Creamy Rice Casserole | 245 | 11 | 600 | 18 | 18 | 50 | 1 S; 2 VLM; ½ V; 2 F |

❖ Dietary Exchanges: S=Starch  Fr=Fruit  C=Carb/Other  V=Vegetable  M=Milk(whole)  F=Fat  VLM=Very Lean Meat  LM=Lean Meat  MFM=Medium-Fat Meat  HFM=High-Fat Meat

| | Calories | Fat (g) | Sodium (mg) | Protein (mg) | Carbohydrate (mg) | Cholesterol (mg) | Exchanges # |
|---|---|---|---|---|---|---|---|
| Danish Pickled Duck | 40 | 2 | 110 | 4 | .5 | 15 | 1 LM |
| Deviled Birds | 713 | 47 | 1,090 | 53 | 17 | 235 | 1 S; 7 LM; 5 F |
| Doves in Corn Bread Stuffing | 621 | 35 | 1,460 | 24 | 53 | 110 | 3½ S; 2 LM; 5½ F |
| Dried Mushroom Sauce (1 Tbsp.) | 21 | 2 | 35 | .2 | 1 | 5 | ½ F |
| Duck and Pistachio Terrine (⅛ recipe) | 325 | 23 | 550 | 24 | 4 | 120 | ½ S; ½ LM; 3 V; 2½ F |
| Duck Breasts with Bacon and Onions | 607 | 48 | 500 | 30 | 8 | 145 | 2½ MFM; ½ F |
| Duck in Corn Bread Stuffing | 475 | 18 | 1,460 | 25 | 53 | 95 | 3½ S; 2 VLM; 3 F |
| Duck with Orange Sauce | 670 | 49 | 680 | 30 | 27 | 140 | ½ Fr; 1½ C; 4 MFM; ½ V; 6 F |
| Duck-Breast Rumaki | 110 | 9 | 140 | 4 | 1 | 20 | ½ S; 4 MFM; 1 V; 5½ F |
| Easy Velouté Sauce (1 Tbsp.) | 30 | 3 | 100 | .3 | 1 | 10 | 1 F |
| Elk Tenderloin Sauté * | 289 | 11 | 1,150 | 30 | 16 | 75 | ½ S; 3½ VLM; 2 V; 2 F |
| Fillet of Venison (5.25 oz.) | 227 | 9 | 105 | 35 | 0 | 135 | 5 VLM; 1½ F |
| Florentine Rabbit Pasta | 650 | 37 | 210 | 26 | 53 | 175 | 2 S; 3 VLM; 7 F |
| Fried Deer Heart Slices | | | | Nutritional information not available | | | |
| Garlic Sausage (4 oz.) | 181 | 11 | 640 | 19 | .4 | 70 | 2½ VLM; 2 F |
| Gingered Rice Stuffing (½ c.) | 154 | 10 | 150 | 2 | 16 | 25 | 1 S; 1 V; 2 F |
| Goose and Wild Rice Casserole | 385 | 22 | 920 | 21 | 26 | 80 | 1½ S; 2½ LM; 1 V; 3 F |
| Goose in Gravy * | 329 | 18 | 200 | 31 | 7 | 105 | ½ S; 4 LM; ½ V; 1½ F |
| Grilled Antelope Shoulder | 223 | 13 | 95 | 25 | .5 | 110 | 4 VLM; 2 F |
| Grilled Bacon-Wrapped Big Game | 207 | 8 | 200 | 32 | .1 | 115 | 4½ VLM; 1 F |
| Grilled Loin with Brown Sugar Baste | 233 | 7 | 440 | 34 | 5 | 135 | 5 VLM; ⅓ C; 1 F |
| Grilled Marinated Pheasants | 788 | 47 | 160 | 83 | 2 | 260 | 12 LM; 2½ F |
| Grilled Teal | 377 | 25 | 60 | 16 | 25 | 60 | 1½ S; 2 LM; ½ V; 3½ F |
| Hasenpfeffer | 454 | 25 | 680 | 41 | 14 | 170 | ½ S; 5½ VLM; 1½ V; 4½ F |
| Hearty Venison Bake | 518 | 39 | 860 | 27 | 15 | 200 | 1 S; 3½ VLM; 1 V; 7 F |
| Homesteaders' Rabbit or Squirrel w/ Cream Gravy | 489 | 27 | 840 | 49 | 11 | 205 | ½ S; 6½ VLM; 1½ V; 4½ F |
| Hot-Smoked Venison Roast | 202 | 7 | 150 | 32 | 0 | 115 | 4½ VLM; 1 F |
| Hungarian Huns | 574 | 29 | 500 | 52 | 25 | 155 | 1 S; ½ Fr; 6½ LM; 2 V; 2 F |
| Hunter's Favorite Chili | 528 | 30 | 950 | 34 | 30 | 125 | 1½ S; 4 VLM; 2 V; 5½ F |
| Italian Green Sauce (1 Tbsp.) | 77 | 8 | 30 | .4 | 1 | 20 | 2 F |
| Italian Meatballs and Sauce* | 492 | 31 | 1,640 | 21 | 33 | 105 | 1 S; 2 VLM; 3½ V; 5½ F |
| Limerick Goose with Potatoes | 592 | 31 | 780 | 37 | 39 | 125 | 2½ S; 4 MFM; ½ V; 2 F |
| Louisiana Boiled Duck | 218 | 16 | 850 | 18 | 0 | 80 | 2½ MFM; ½ F |
| Madeira Game Sauce (1 Tbsp.) | 35 | 2 | 75 | .3 | 3 | 5 | ½ S; ½ F |
| Mandarin Duck Salad | 316 | 26 | 160 | 9 | 14 | 25 | ½ Fr; 1 LM; 1½ V; 4½ F |
| Mandarin Goose | 596 | 36 | 125 | 41 | 26 | 150 | 1 Fr; 1 C; 6 MFM; 1 F |
| Mexican Chorizo Sausage (4 oz.) | 209 | 12 | 500 | 23 | 1 | 90 | 3½ VLM; 2 F |
| Mexican Enchilada Casserole | 448 | 31 | 730 | 26 | 17 | 110 | 1 S; 3 VLM; 1½ V; 6 F |
| Mississippi Duck Gumbo* | 219 | 13 | 800 | 10 | 17 | 30 | 4½ LM; 1 C; ½ V; 4 F |
| Northwoods Duck and Wild Rice | 454 | 31 | 270 | 19 | 24 | 90 | 1½ S; 3 F; 2 HFM |
| Old-Fashioned Venison Stew | 350 | 9 | 490 | 35 | 30 | 120 | ½ S; 4 VLM; ½ C; 4 V; 1½ F |
| Onion-Bread Dressing | 142 | 9 | 490 | 3 | 13 | 35 | 1 S; ½ V; 2 F |

* Rice, noodles, or toast not included in analysis.

| | Calories | Fat (g) | Sodium (mg) | Protein (mg) | Carbohydrate (mg) | Cholesterol (mg) | Exchanges ❖ |
|---|---|---|---|---|---|---|---|
| Orange Onion Liver | | | | Nutritional information not available | | | |
| Orange-Flavored Brown Sauce (1 Tbsp.) | 31 | 2 | 75 | .3 | 2 | 5 | ½ F |
| Oriental Pheasant Salad | 260 | 13 | 120 | 16 | 20 | 50 | ½ S; 2½ VLM; 1 Fr; 2 F |
| Oriental-Style Grilled Venison Ribs | 233 | 7 | 520 | 34 | 7 | 125 | 5 VLM; ½ C; 1 F |
| Oven-Barbecued Rabbit | 439 | 13 | 870 | 48 | 33 | 195 | 6 VLM; 1 C; 4 V; 2 F |
| Oven-Barbecued Venison Ribs | 268 | 4 | 1,090 | 35 | 23 | 125 | 5 VLM; 1½ C; ½ F |
| Oven-Braised Rabbit with Gravy | 403 | 15 | 710 | 49 | 16 | 180 | ½ S; 6½ VLM; 2 V; 2 F |
| Partridge Newburg* | 252 | 16 | 380 | 17 | 8 | 145 | 2 LM; ½ C; ½ M; ½ V; 2 F |
| Pepper-Flavored Brown Sauce (1 Tbsp.) | 31 | 2 | 75 | .3 | 1 | 5 | ½ V; ½ F |
| Peppered Antelope Roast (4 oz.) | 208 | 10 | 150 | 27 | .1 | 115 | 4 VLM; 2 F |
| Pheasant in Creamy Mushroom Sauce | 681 | 40 | 920 | 59 | 17 | 185 | 1 S; 8 LM; 1½ V; 3 F |
| Pheasant Paprika* | 680 | 48 | 1,170 | 44 | 16 | 170 | 1 S; 6 LM; 6 F |
| Pheasant Picatta with Morels | 498 | 26 | 510 | 39 | 24 | 140 | 1½ S; 5 VLM; ½ M; 4 F |
| Pheasant with Apples | 709 | 42 | 540 | 57 | 23 | 230 | 1 Fr; 8 LM; 1½ V; 4 F |
| "Poached" Wild Goose | 589 | 43 | 150 | 48 | 0 | 175 | 7 MFM; 2 F |
| Polynesian Roast Duck | 556 | 24 | 670 | 27 | 56 | 110 | 1½ S; 1 Fr; 3½ LM; 1½ C; ½ V; 3 F |
| Potato Sausage (4 oz.) | 156 | 6 | 480 | 13 | 11 | 60 | 1 S; 1½ VLM; 1 F |
| Quail Grilled in Cabbage Leaves | 777 | 61 | 460 | 51 | 5 | 275 | 7 LM; 1 V; 8 F |
| Quail in Corn Bread Stuffing | 734 | 37 | 1,520 | 45 | 53 | 175 | 3½ S; 5 LM; 4 F |
| Quail with Port Wine Sauce (2 birds) | 633 | 38 | 810 | 51 | 18 | 215 | ½ S; 7 LM; 1 C; 3½ F |
| Quick Venison-Rotini Soup | 290 | 12 | 810 | 16 | 30 | 50 | 2 S; 1½ VLM; 1 V; 2 F |
| Rabbit Braised with Bacon and Mushrooms | 579 | 28 | 1,010 | 54 | 24 | 215 | 1 S; 7 VLM; ½ Fr; 1 V; 5 F |
| Rabbit in Apple Cider | 472 | 14 | 550 | 48 | 39 | 180 | 6½ VLM; 2 Fr; 2 V; 2 F |
| Rabbit Pot Pie | 518 | 32 | 330 | 27 | 31 | 150 | 2 S; 3 VLM; ½ V; 6 F |
| Rabbit Salad | 233 | 15 | 390 | 18 | 6 | 170 | 2½ VLM; 1 V; 3 F |
| Rabbit Stew | 557 | 28 | 1,240 | 50 | 27 | 170 | 5½ VLM; 5½ V; 5 F |
| Rabbit with Dumplings | 797 | 40 | 1,710 | 59 | 48 | 280 | 3½ S; 7 VLM; 6½ F |
| Raccoon with Sauerkraut | | | | Nutritional information not available | | | |
| Roast Big Game Tenderloin (4 oz.) | 143 | 6 | 160 | 16 | 5 | 45 | ½ S; 2½ VLM; 1 F |
| Roast Boneless Sirloin Tip (4 oz.) | 159 | 5 | 60 | 26 | 0 | 100 | 3½ VLM; 1 F |
| Roast Goose with Baked Apples | 752 | 45 | 240 | 49 | 38 | 180 | ½ S; 1½ Fr; 1 C; 7 MFM; 2 F |
| Roast Lemon-Mint Duck | 582 | 47 | 930 | 35 | 8 | 200 | ½ Fr; 5 LM; 6½ F |
| Roast Pheasant with Sauerkraut | 760 | 52 | 1,400 | 59 | 5 | 235 | 8 LM; 1 V; 5½ F |
| Roast Wild Turkey (⅛ recipe using 12-lb. bird) | 831 | 38 | 320 | 110 | 5 | 325 | 15½ VLM; ½ V; 6 F |
| Rolled Stuffed Roast of Venison | 341 | 12 | 430 | 48 | 6 | 175 | ½ S; 6½ VLM; ½ V; 2 F |
| Ruffed Grouse Strips in Butter | 126 | 8 | 80 | 13 | 0 | 55 | 2 VLM; 1½ F |
| Sautéed Partridge Breast with Figs | 824 | 51 | 890 | 55 | 38 | 240 | 2½ Fr; 8 LM; 5½ F |
| Savory Pineapple-Baked Quail | 587 | 31 | 220 | 50 | 27 | 190 | 2 Fr; 7 LM; 2 F |
| Savory Pot Pie | 515 | 33 | 350 | 24 | 31 | 120 | 2 S; 3 VLM; ½ V; 6 F |
| Sesame Duck Cabbage Salad | 211 | 14 | 340 | 9 | 14 | 25 | 1 LM; 3 V; 2 F |
| Sharptail on Mushroom Toast | 503 | 32 | 610 | 30 | 20 | 125 | 1 S; 3½ LM; 1 V; 4½ F |
| Sherried Squirrel or Rabbit | 385 | 16 | 1,280 | 47 | 9 | 185 | ½ S; 6½ VLM; ½ C; ½ V; 2½ F |

❖ Dietary Exchanges: S=Starch  Fr=Fruit  C=Carb/Other  V=Vegetable  M=Milk(whole)  F=Fat  VLM=Very Lean Meat  LM=Lean Meat  MFM=Medium-Fat Meat  HFM=High-Fat Meat

| | Calories | Fat (g) | Sodium (mg) | Protein (mg) | Carbohydrate (mg) | Cholesterol | Exchanges # |
|---|---|---|---|---|---|---|---|
| Skillet Game Hash | 248 | 9 | 360 | 18 | 24 | 60 | 2 S; 2 VLM; 1½ F |
| Smoky Canned Big-Game Chunks (⅙ recipe) | 326 | 10 | 920 | 52 | 3 | 190 | 7½ VLM; 1½ F |
| Smothered Birds | 709 | 47 | 1,090 | 53 | 16 | 235 | 1 S; 7 LM; 5 F |
| Southern Fried Squirrel or Rabbit with Gravy | 567 | 29 | 660 | 51 | 22 | 190 | 1½ S; 7 VLM; 5 F |
| Spanish Rabbit | 736 | 26 | 1,770 | 55 | 70 | 170 | 3 S; 5 VLM; 6 V; 4½ F |
| Spicy Duck Stir-Fry with Peanuts* | 477 | 32 | 1,390 | 33 | 14 | 100 | ½ MFM; ½ V; 1½ F |
| Spicy Elk Kabobs | 161 | 3.5 | 280 | 27 | 4 | 60 | 3½ VLM; 1 V; ½ F |
| Spicy Sausage Dressing (½ c.) | 233 | 18 | 340 | 5 | 14 | 30 | 1 S; ½ V; 3 F; ½ HFM |
| Stewed Partridge with Sage Dumplings | 433 | 13 | 1,300 | 41 | 37 | 120 | 2 S; 4½ VLM; 2 V; 2 F |
| Stuffed Breasts of Grouse | 579 | 32 | 1,520 | 38 | 33 | 170 | 2 S; 4½ VLM; ½ V; 5½ F |
| Stuffed Roast Goose | 837 | 43 | 520 | 48 | 56 | 165 | 3 S; 1 Fr; 5½ MFM; 3 F |
| Sunday Roast Grouse with Dressing | | | (see Sunday Roast Pheasant with Dressing) | | | | |
| Sunday Roast Partridge with Dressing | | | (see Sunday Roast Pheasant with Dressing) | | | | |
| Sunday Roast Pheasant with Dressing | 777 | 45 | 1,750 | 51 | 38 | 230 | 2½ S; 6 LM; 1 V; 5½ F |
| Swedish Meatballs with Brown Gravy | 294 | 21 | 930 | 17 | 7 | 115 | ½ S; 2½ VLM; 4 F |
| Sweet Italian Sausage (4 oz.) | 207 | 12 | 540 | 23 | 1 | 90 | 3½ VLM; 2 F |
| Texas-Style Venison Chili* | 196 | 6 | 340 | 19 | 17 | 65 | ½ S; 2 VLM; 2½ V; 1 F |
| Tomato-Rabbit Casserole | 571 | 14 | 1,050 | 54 | 57 | 180 | 2 S; 5½ VLM; 5½ V; 2 F |
| Traditional Venison Jerky (1 oz.) | 70 | 1.5 | 670 | 13 | .4 | 50 | 2 VLM |
| Turkey and Dressing Casserole | 322 | 20 | 780 | 19 | 17 | 85 | 1 S; 2½ VLM; ½ V; 3½ F |
| Turkey Lentil Soup | 144 | 3 | 870 | 16 | 14 | 25 | 1 S; 2 VLM; ½ V; ½ F |
| Tuscan Hare with Pasta*† | 364 | 16 | 1,110 | 39 | 16 | 135 | 5 VLM; 3 V; 3 F |
| Upland Birds in Oven Cooking Bag | 585 | 34 | 220 | 56 | 10 | 205 | ½ Fr; 8 LM; 2 F |
| Upland Stir-Fry* | 313 | 16 | 660 | 21 | 20 | 115 | 1 S; 2 VLM; 1 V; 3 F |
| Vegetable Quail Casserole | 721 | 47 | 920 | 53 | 20 | 235 | 1½ S; 7 LM; ½ V; 5½ F |
| Venison and Beans | 376 | 18 | 880 | 21 | 36 | 70 | 2 S; 2½ VLM; ½ C; 3 F |
| Venison Breakfast Sausage (4 oz.) | 250 | 18 | 520 | 20 | .2 | 85 | 3 VLM; 3½ F |
| Venison Heart Roast | | | Nutritional information not available | | | | |
| Venison Liver Pâté | | | Nutritional information not available | | | | |
| Venison Meatball Pot Pie | 572 | 35 | 1,050 | 22 | 45 | 105 | 3 S; 2 VLM; 6½ F |
| Venison Meatloaf Supreme | 362 | 25 | 490 | 24 | 8 | 155 | ½ S; 3 VLM; 1 V; 4½ F |
| Venison Mincemeat (¼ c.) | 175 | 6 | 95 | 4 | 30 | 15 | ½ VLM; 1½ Fr; ½ C; 1 F |
| Venison Picatta | 407 | 17 | 660 | 37 | 17 | 160 | 1 S; 5 VLM; ½ C; ½ M; 3 F |
| Venison Roast Burgundy | 284 | 5 | 260 | 47 | 10 | 170 | 6 VLM; 2 V; ½ F |
| Venison Sauerbraten | 366 | 7 | 790 | 52 | 23 | 180 | 1 S; 6 VLM; 2 V; ½ F |
| Venison Steak Diane | 423 | 22 | 430 | 46 | 2 | 215 | 7 VLM; 4 F |
| Venison Stroganoff* | 303 | 16 | 540 | 26 | 11 | 115 | ½ S; 3½ VLM; 1 V; 3 F |
| Venison Vegetable Soup (1 c.) | 87 | 2.5 | 540 | 9 | 8 | 35 | ½ S; 1 VLM; 1 V; ½ F |
| Wild Turkey Picatta with Morels | 635 | 24 | 610 | 77 | 24 | 240 | 1½ S; 10 VLM; ½ M; 3 F |
| Wine-Braised Duck | 483 | 38 | 420 | 21 | 14 | 90 | 1 S; 2 MFM; 1 V; 5 F |
| Woodcock in Chablis | 396 | 16 | 700 | 46 | 9 | 150 | ½ S; 6½ VLM; ½ C; 1 V; 2 F |
| Zesty Venison Stew | 301 | 8 | 790 | 30 | 28 | 95 | 1½ S; 3 VLM; ½ C; 1 V; 1 F |

* Rice, noodles, or toast not included in analysis.     † Analysis uses nutritional information for wild rabbit.

# Index

159

Creative Publishing international, Inc.
offers a variety of how-to books.
For information write:
  Creative Publishing international, Inc.
  Subscriber Books
  5900 Green Oak Drive
  Minnetonka, MN 55343